How to Pray
without being
Religious

How to Pray
without being
Religious

Finding Your Own Spiritual Path

Janell Moon

 element

Element
An Imprint of HarperCollins*Publishers*
77–85 Fulham Palace Road,
Hammersmith, London W6 8JB

The website address is: www.thorsonselement.com

 ™

and *Element* are trademarks of
HarperCollins*Publishers* Ltd

First published by Thorsons 2004

10 9 8 7 6 5 4 3 2 1

© Janell Moon, 2004

Janell Moon asserts the moral right to
be identified as the author of this work

The author's website address is: www.janellmoon.com

A catalogue record of this book
is available from the British Library

ISBN 0 00 717485 3

Printed and bound in U.S.A.

❧

Contents

Part Three: Prayers for Living Your Dreams

Part Four: Tipping the Balance

To Matthew, a precious new spirit on Earth with us.

Acknowledgments

I'd like to thank my family and friends for all their support as I wrote this prayer book. Special thanks to Linda Roghaar, my agent, for finding it a home; Greg Brandenburgh, the publisher, for understanding the importance of what I was saying; and Caroline Pincus for being the best editor ever. Ongoing thanks to Lonnie Hull Dupont and Jan Johnson for believing in me and starting it all.

❦

Introduction

I am the wind that gathers upon the sea; I am the wave; the murmur of billows. I am a beam of sun; the fairest of plants; I am a wild boar in valor; an ox in combat. I am a salmon in the water; a lake on the plain; I am a word of truth; a point on the lance of battle. I am the spark that creates fire in the head.

THE MYSTERY OF AMERIGIN, IRELAND, C.1700 BC

Why Are We Gathered Here?

❦

Have you ever had one of those days when everything just shines gloriously and you have a feeling that all is well, and you find a *thank you* bursting inside your heart? Perhaps a window of vision opened as you were relaxing near a river and you sensed that you belonged to everything: the river, the bird, its song. This moment showed you that you could transform life by holding on to the oneness of all sentient beings.

Have you ever hit a brick wall in a friendship and felt helpless and alone? Did you ever long to hear in your beloved's voice a softening tone that echoes your newfound forgiveness, "It's okay. We'll be fine"? It is in moments like these that we find the heart of prayer.

More and more of us are discovering that prayer doesn't have to be about church, though sometimes we find prayer's heart there, too. We are praying, but we're not praying in the old ways.

Perhaps you go to church or temple regularly and pray with the congregation but find yourself using prayer in your daily life, too – to connect with the spirit, to seek guidance, to express what's in your heart.

Perhaps you pray to your own gods or goddesses or the Great Spirit, and are finding that by connecting with spirit, you are feeling joined to the whole human (and nonhuman) global community.

Perhaps you were brought up going to church but left because it didn't seem right for you. Maybe you began to have trouble with the teachings or couldn't hold the teachings as true given what was going on in your family and you fled the church, your religious associations still braided with painful memories. Perhaps you left because you felt that the church's stand against birth control or divorce or homosexuality was too large an issue to overlook.

Or perhaps you were just too gloriously young to sit and listen and wiggled your way free to the green grass outside.

Some of us left our childhood churches in rebellion against the way religion was used as a way to control our yearning to question and explore. Others were introduced to some religious teachings as kids but they never seemed important until we became older or experienced a crisis. And then we found that the formal teachings simply didn't feed our spirits. But we still carry with us the longing to pray.

Others of us were not brought up with any religion at all, often because our parents had been hurt by their own religious upbringing and chose to be free of all that, raising their families to believe in peace and love. But the ideas of love and peace may not have given us a strong enough structure from which to pray and we now find that we need something more.

Some of us enjoy the occasional visit to an ashram or church or temple or we may like to chant with a group. Some of us meditate. We may feel blessed when we have a chance to walk an ancient labyrinth but we return to the harbor of our homes to continue to practice our faith. Some of us still go to church, taking what we need and leaving the rest. With this new path to spirit, we create more of what we need, which allows us to better embrace prayer.

No, we no longer have to compromise ourselves by praying in the church that held safe the nun that hit us. We don't have to try to take the sexist culture out of Buddhism to make it a more welcoming home for our practice. We don't have to pretend we believe in only one God, only one way. We are discovering that we can have a prayer life that we can believe in wholly, a connection to spirit that we can totally embrace.

But how do we pray in such an unchurched context? What do our prayers sound like? What do we say? How do we find a spiritual path that binds us to the heart of things and a prayer life that gives us the opportunity to develop deep knowledge of our true selves?

As we look for prayers that connect us to spirit, that light our path, that reflect our deep desire for a sense of rootedness on this earth, we find ourselves without maps.

I wrote *How to Pray Without Being Religious* to give voice to this longing for prayer and to share with you the personal prayers that help me keep my connection to spirit. Some prayers I wrote:

> **Blessed be. A place for me.**

Others I gathered:

> **Look, I see the Sun. He is my father. He is my beginning.**
> **Look, I see the Moon ... She is my Grandmother. My**
> **guardian keeper. Look, I see the stars ... They are my**
> **friends, my relatives. Look, I see the universe. I see myself.**
> > (HIGH EAGLE, OSAGE/CHEROKEE TRIBES)

I will share them with you in the pages that follow.

A Yearning for Truth

In his book *Contemplative Prayer,* progressive Christian monk Thomas Merton writes, "In the prayer of the heart we seek first of all the deepest ground of our identity ... We seek to gain a direct existential grasp, a personal experience of the deepest truths of life and faith, finding ourselves in truth." Our new prayers are prayers of the heart, in which we find our way to our own deepest truths.

A Yearning for Connection

As we begin to focus our prayers on the truth of our lives, we begin to notice much to be thankful for: good health, the beautiful day, loving friends. We can become aware of what areas we can improve whether it be traits in ourselves or relationships with others. We can learn to accept and let go of anger, greed, and jealousy. We can discover that we have more tolerance, learn to live more simply, and find a generosity toward ourselves and others. As we find ourselves troubled, we can pray to be released from the webbed cage of fear and separation. We may continue to have troubles but we will not *be* troubled, not in the same way. Prayer allows us to spring open the steel doors and walk out into the light.

The personal prayers you'll find here, and those you will create, and those you will begin to hear around you, affirm that we can live in awareness of ourselves as unique creatures in the universe. We each have our own DNA and fingerprints. We have encoded in us many gifts and have the potential to develop many talents. Prayer helps us discover ourselves as both small and mighty, acorn and oak.

We who see that not everyone is given equal breaks and opportunities can use prayer for the courage to open our hearts with compassion. As we recognize our own feelings of deprivation, we can pray to lessen this feeling by longing for generosity. We can pray for the changing of the world back to a people bound to their connection to themselves, aware that the wind also gives us life.

Developing Inclusive Prayers

In Patricia Lynn Reilly's *A God Who Looks Like Me: Discovering A Woman-Affirming Spirituality*, she offers this vision of creation:

> "In the beginning was the Mother. On the first day she gave birth to light and darkness. They danced together. On the second day she gave birth to land and water. They touched. On the third day she gave birth to the plants. They grew roots and breathed. On the fourth day she gave birth to land, sea, and air creatures. They walked and flew and swam. On the fifth day her creation learned balance and cooperation. She thanked her partner for coaching her labor. On the sixth day she celebrated the creativity of all living things. On the seventh day she left space for the unknown."

I wonder now what it would have been like to have been told that there was a divine feminine within me that had wisdom I could follow all the days of my life; that she just needed to be fed with the quiet of prayer and kindness in action. I could have prayed to the Wise Woman, Lilith, the Divine Girl, or the Mother-Who-Walks-With-the-Earth. I would have felt included, and that inclusion could have helped me in my growing up and difficult teen years. I could have asked for wisdom from the depths within. I could have become comfortable and not fearful, right from the start, with the unknown.

By naming our own gods or spirits we remind ourselves that we are taking charge of our own lives and we present a vision to all children of a world in which girls are included in the mystery of all that we can feel but cannot see. By naming our own gods or spirits we pioneer a new way of faith that includes ourselves.

We've been accommodating for too long: ignoring sexist language, overlooking God as *he*, understanding that the word *man* in poetry, literature, and religion is said to include women even if we are never mentioned. We have been called upon to overlook sexist, racist, classist, homophobic sentiment and language in the Bible, in Greek myths, in all the classic plays and literature. Now it's our time. We want to pray with language that reflects our deepest values, positive, inclusive language that embraces all beings as equals:

Let me embrace what I believe with others at my side. All of it.

Finding Our Own Way

Together we who seek direct connection with spirit are forming a new culture – one that values kindness and love and simplicity, one that honors the earth and its sentient beings:

Each, belongs. A new welcoming.

This book is my offering to this ever-widening circle.

We know that praying in the new way is just as valid as having a minister or rabbi or master, a congregation, the whole of a sanga praying with us; we are praying with the wisest energy in our lives, with our belief in spirit, and that is enough. But sometimes we could use some encouragement.

A client of mine was bought up as a Catholic and loved the music in the cathedral of his childhood. He was drawn to transcendental meditation in the 1960s and used a tone given to him as a mantra for many years. He traveled to Kentucky to meditate with Trungpa Rinpoche's rural community for several years. He spent time with the pagan Reclaiming Community in California learning of the earth Mother. He tells me that after all these years he still feels he hasn't found the path he wanted, and yet as I listen to him I hear a real friendship with a godlike energy that has allowed him to author many books and teach in universities around the world. What he hasn't found is *one* way as he thought he would; instead, he followed an inner path that winds through many religions. I offer him this:

God, Buddha, Allah, Goddess, Father/Mother Spirit, lead me to gardens holding pools of water.

He tells me he shortens the salutation to: Old Wise One. He tried Holy One but that felt too holy:

Old Wise One, lead me to gardens holding pools of water.

Another client of mine studies with a Hindu master and medi-
tates and prays to the Jesus of her South Carolina childhood.
When she told her master that she prays to Jesus, he said, "Ah,
Jesus. Yes." She reads Buddhist books and comes to me for
direction concerning her relationship with her Jewish husband.
These personal prayers are for her, too.

We can find our own way. I know a young woman from
Vietnam who was afraid of the Buddhist temples of her childhood
because her family believed ghosts lived in them. Then she found
herself praying but without the ritual she loved from Buddhism.
Now she does personal prayer with a spirit house she created. It
looks like a tiny bird house. She says it keeps the unfriendly
ghosts at a safe distance. Inside she places offerings to the ghosts
of a shiny coin and ribbons of beauty and prays to her spirit:

*Let this tiny house hold the sadness of the world. Help me
find connection and peace.*

How to Voice Personal Prayer

What are we doing here wondering about praying without a religious orientation? Thinking of praying not connected to a church
or its community? We're including ourselves in the prayer of the
world, praying in a new way that comes from spontaneous feelings of the heart. Call it a new prayer, call it personal prayer, it is
an outpouring of what we most deeply feel and just as the roots
of a tree stretch to ground the tree and search for nourishment,

so does new prayer take us to solid places with which we are unfamiliar and there we find nourishment:

I am included in all things. Thank you, dear spirit, for holding hope while I learn to trust my heart.

We pray for the joining of all things, the spirit that lives in the world with the spirit of the heart. We give prayers of wonder and thanksgiving, we find our prayers of longing rising from our animal bodies, and we voice a need for transformation in acceptance and action:

I give praise for the little feet of love around the world. Lift me to the light in the trees. Let me begin with acceptance and end with transformation. Footprints and sand, together, earthbound prayer.

By stepping into our own spirituality, we engage a quiet part of us, that part of us that knows we are spirit inhabiting a physical body. We develop an even deeper faith in our connection to all living things. We are conscious, therefore, of ourselves as part of the weave of life and turn to this fabric to pray.

We develop faith as a means of letting go of being "right" and letting god or the spirit into the picture to reveal its own mysteries. We turn to the spiritual belief that the day itself brings god and spirit into our hands and that it is the present, here and now, with which we join in conversation.

In this new way of prayer we have no set structure or architecture. However, if we did, it would let in the spirit of the land and the light, much like a Frank Lloyd Wright house.

How I Came to Write This Book

I was brought up in a Christian church. We attended services whenever my mother could talk my atheistic father into sitting through a sermon. I sat in the pews and learned to use prayer as a way to plea bargain with God. How good that felt! The earnestness, the hope. I would beg for help and then forget prayer when circumstances changed. You know, take the good luck offered, perform better on the test, and run. I kept my prayers manageable and small and, in that way, I felt my prayers were often answered. Something like: *Let me make it through the test, or the day, or date. I promise I will never ask for anything again. I promise to study harder.*

I eventually drifted away from the Church, with its prayers of confession or repentance, because it seemed to be such a punishing system. Believing that God and prayer were synonymous, I left prayer behind, too. I no longer wanted to say my deepest yearnings to someone of whom I was afraid.

As a teenager, I read in Anne Frank's diary that, in spite of what the Nazis were doing to her people, she believed that people are basically good. I felt Anne was holding a generous feeling in the open heart of the young. I myself lived in a family of strangers yet sensed my parents meant to love me but did not have the self-knowledge or the ability to be honest about feelings that intimacy required. I wandered through my childhood alone and unsupported and now I saw a vision of openheartedness. From Anne, I now had words for what I believed. I brought prayer back into my life and each night would ask:

Hold me.

Years later, as I toured with my first two books, I found myself at many retreats and churches: prayer was all around me once again. I heard a minister tell his congregation that prayer is not about what you can get but rather a way of relating to your spirit or god. This, I realized, was what I had been doing: praying for a better connection to my spirit. I wanted a relationship with a spirit energy. I wanted to return to the best of what I had experienced as a child sitting on the shores of the Cuyahoga River in Ohio, filling up lined tablet paper with my prayers and not wanting to go to church.

I floundered around for awhile and wrote in my journal. I swam in the deep pools of California, splashed in her waterfalls, and wrote: "Guide me."

I started imagining my next steps and explored how prayer could both help me appreciate the good I had and create a deeper connection to who I was and who I was becoming. I wanted to be reminded of the truth of who I was beyond the writer or worker that was identifying my life. After spending four years writing two books, I felt the need to pray for a vision of what was possible:

Guide me.

And then I became aware that prayer had become a part of my everyday life. I remember one evening in particular. I was on my way to meet a friend to write poetry together, a very rare treat I allowed myself. It had been raining and I noticed the puddles with a feeling of utter contentment. I belonged here.

The wind pushed me around the corner from my office to the coffee house. I could feel the push of the wind as a longing in myself.

I entered the café, its sudden warmth washing over me, and I realized how grateful I was to be there and to be in my life. I looked at the diversity of people sipping their drinks and talking together and felt a deep sense of comfort. Again, grateful. Inside, I crossed my heart as a promise, a prayer, that I would give myself a night in conversation with a friend and poetry more often.

As I left that night, filled with poetry, I also noticed feelings of competition with my poet friend and how swiftly her poems seemed to find strong endings. Mine seemed like fragments of beauty, no end in sight. As I write this now, I smile as I see the symbolism spelled out beneath my fingertips, but at the time I hated admitting my negative feelings in the midst of so much abundance. I wanted to be a better person, a more spiritual person.

As I headed to my car, my umbrella turned inside out from the strength of the wind. I had a minute of struggle and was so cold when I finally did made it to the door. It was late and suddenly I was tired and knew I had to get up early in the morning. I couldn't help but think that that was what I had done for much of my life – struggled in the wind and cold to find meaning.

But lately I felt I had begun living a more imaginative, symbolic life. I'd begun noticing the magical in the everyday. And I'd been having good fortune turning hardship and some depression inside out. Here I was driving home, shivering in the old way but feeling prayerful in the new way. I thought of my spirit:

Raindrop, all I need.

After that evening, I started doing a lot of praying through my journal writing. At first I'd write in a plain-speaking way: Help me find a way to my spirit.

Then I'd get fancy:

I'm blessed with nights of lightning bugs flickering their wand before me, finches bringing messages from departed ones, days when grass glows neon, and the heavens, mirrors of fish and flora in glass lakes.

Gradually I developed a practice of writing my prayers, rereading them, and then praying from the page:

Help me see beyond what I can see. Let me enjoy this clay land and quiet. Spirit, maker, mother, father, me. Thank you for ripe summer.

I started taking these personal prayers into my days, using them as a kind of mantra. These simple lines nourished a hunger for connection. You will find many of my personal prayers sprinkled throughout this book. They come from many sources: from the feelings that I manage to catch hold of as they arise in my heart, from chants, poems, and prayers from native Americans and others who express this human longing to pray to a spirit that is all inclusive.

As you find ways to give thanks, ask for help, and envision change, as you look for ways to nurture the spirit of generosity in yourself and the world, the instinct to pray will come even more alive in you.

You can use the instinct of prayer to pray the feeling of the heart with all its love and longing and vision of a better world. You can call on the spirit of the heart to fill your day with prayer:

Heart, spirit, let me be with you.

Even back in the days when I was less aware of my spirit, I had the instinct to pray. I remember walking in a redwood forest at the Russian River one day and seeing a gentle light shining through to the forest floor much like a beam of the divine asking to be noticed and I stood with a prayer in my body:

Yes.

Years before, I'd walk down Chestnut Street in my home town of Cuyahoga Falls, Ohio, on my way to high school, the trees forming a cathedral over my head, and sigh the big sigh:

Beauty, everywhere.

This is what the new prayer is all about.

I remember when my son and his wife showed me the sonogram of their first child, a tiny human forming in the womb of love. Right then I could feel their love, my love for them, and the fragility of human life. I knew that the spirit was in the room with us right alongside the everyday: the clicking on and off of the furnace, the stack of hand-me-down baby clothes on the old blue chair I had given them, the pile of papers to sort, the cat soaking up the sun. I sensed that everything was as it should be, spirit alive. In instinct, a prayer:

Love.

The unexpected smile of the woman behind a counter, the neighbor who takes in a package for me, the man at the four-way stop who waves me on even when it's his right of way. A therapy client telling me that kindness made her want to live. Just to be in her presence makes me a vehicle for prayer:

Thank you.

I pray in order to express the truth of my place in the universe, a person who will live awhile and then die, life lived each day in the presence of the infinite mystery, unfolding and finite in time.

As we invent a new way to pray, we join a body of people who want prayer to reflect their experiences and values. We bring prayer to our heart as our hand brings food to the mouth. We repeat our prayers because each time we pray we get closer to our spirit:

I am wanted in prayer.

Prayer is coming to us and saying that we matter; it is offering us a gift. Prayer offers a home to believers and doubters alike, to anyone who wants guidance, to give thanks, or to clarify visions.

What You Will Find in the Pages Ahead

Throughout this book I want to help you hear prayer's whisper. I have divided it into four parts. *Prayers of Wonder* express the music of our heart of how we love our life and our world and all living things. *Prayers of Possibility* give voice to our human yearnings: our hopes and dreams for ourselves, all others, and the breathing earth. We know we can ask for what we want and will be heard. We listen for answers within our daily life. With *Prayers for Living Your Dreams*, we take the leap to believing that we can put an energy into the world that can create change for the better. We search for a vision, and for it we pray. I invite you to add your own as they come to you and together we will invent a new prayer tradition. *Tipping the Balance*, the fourth section, brings prayer and social justice together as we explore how to combine the political with the personal and create a life of prayer with action.

As I see it, prayer is a natural human condition. Left to our own devices, we'll find our way to it. Just as the body needs rest and the mind needs peace, the spirit needs attention. If we will just notice, the spirit will bring us to the marrow of ourselves:

Spirit, in me shine.

It is my hope that this book will help you use prayer as an opportunity to live. Because one of the promises of prayer is to bring us closer to life as it is, we learn through prayer to accept life on its own terms. We cease the struggle to have life follow our will and allow ourselves to be part of a divine plan of which we may not see the whole. We learn through prayer to trust that all we need to do is put our best energy into the mix of things:

May the best be done.

Let us lean into these personal prayers for shelter and a way to practice our spiritual life. Pray for the acceptance of the self who is afraid to risk, pray for the energy to begin and believe again, pray for guidance so that you might find more of your aliveness. As our world becomes more technical, I pray and write:

May we find deep meaning in life that lives at our fingertips. Just look at our hands, they are ablaze!

PART ONE

Prayers of Wonder

Thank you for the quiet of the day.
I am not alone.
All of us, new song of earth.

We start with prayers of wonder because it is one of our most natural instincts to want to say thank you to life. As we feel connected to the spirit of all things, as we become aware that we are being enfolded in a physical life of self, loved ones, and the treasured earth, we may want to offer a prayer. We may want to offer thanksgiving that we are asked to participate as a part of the whole of our time.

CHAPTER 1

❧

Saying Thank You

Thank you for my life.
Thank you for all, here with me.
Thank you for my part in the whole.

Many people speak of wanting to express their gratitude for abundance, for the fact that they have enough. We can look inside our hearts and see what good is overflowing in our lives. We can look outside the window and know that the earth ground is great and a part of us, the sunflower waving its vibrant beauty as an affirmation of life.

One Sunday evening, after a weekend in nature, I wrote this poem:

Offering
The earth's quiet body welcomes us
to her granite slabs
above the cooling pans of stone quarries,
shade of her sweet gum tree.
"I have enough. I have been given much."
We slow down cut and foliage,

offer rows of fertile resting,
any ocean of need
sated by wheat in her arms.

And from the poem I took a single line in prayer:

I have been given much.

I then brought that prayer line into my week by writing it in my daily calendar book under Monday. Whenever I saw it, I was reminded to be grateful. A little trick like writing a prayer line down in a place you'll see it often helps you remember you are alive beyond your tied-shoe day.

During a recent trip in the south, I watched a sapsucker with a yellow belly use her tail to steady its crawl up a tree trunk until it got to where it wanted to tap for the insect life under the bark. I knew she was after nourishment for her trip back to the north. She was here awhile and then gone and I was nourished just to watch her antics. I said a little prayer:

Life, and all its tiny moments. Thank you.

There is a line by poet William Blake that says that "We are put on earth for a little space that we may learn to bear the beams of love." We can create prayers of wonder to show our love and, in this act, learn to love more deeply:

There is everything here for me.

I have a neighbor whose life is filled with spirit. I don't exactly know what she does for a living but I see her every day after work, out in her container garden puttering, if even for only a few minutes. She keeps notes in a small journal book on what the alligator ferns, yellow lilies, azaleas, rhododendron, and trumpet flowers need. She waters her herbs: parsley, onion, garlic, lemon and lime thyme, basil, oregano, and peppermint. She picks out herbs for dinner and puts the peppermint in covered water jars to keep in the sun for tea. She stakes the vegetables and sits outside on her wrought iron chair with a shaker of salt eating tomatoes.

I catch glimpses of her as I write at my window across the courtyard, and am impressed at her level of concentration and the sense of her contentment. I think, what a spiritual way to spend the last light of the day. She is being prayer, she tells me, but she also prays to the spirit. She says that patio gardening is the only time she isn't thinking of work or family concerns and she wouldn't give up time on this tiny piece of land for anything. I notice she's out there earlier and earlier each year and write this prayer:

Haven of my day.

"I don't know how I *couldn't* pray, the spirit is so alive in my garden," she reminds me. And I remember a friend saying that her garden is the closest she can come to being present to creation.

As we begin to notice the natural world and pray in prayers of wonder, we find that change can be in our own gardens. In *The Botany of Desire*, Michael Pollan traces the potential of a garden to act with the power to alter experience, "There's an older idea of the garden, back before the popularity for flowers, of powerful plants that change us – that heal us, or poison, do all these things we don't discuss anymore." He speaks of growing medicinal herbs such as St John's Wort and valerian for calming teas and exploring what wonder you can bring to yourself. I jot down a prayer:

Wonder, I notice and create.

A client of mine who is doing well with a chronic illness tells me of an old saying from Tibet, "When the conch shell is blocked, the best way to clear it is to blow into it." She puts energy into her negative feelings and with their release finds it easier to focus on the positive. She writes lists of gratitude because it helps her mood. She tries to focus on what she has, not what she doesn't have:

Thank you for life.

"I have never found it easy to give praise, perhaps because I wasn't praised as a child, the habit doesn't come to me naturally. I had to learn how to do this when I was teaching children in inner city public school and it was so apparent how much the students needed validation. I could do it for them and in time it became a bit easier," she relates to me. "Giving thanks was a quick habit of saying, 'Thank you,' but to say more than that seemed gushy. Now that I'm ill and have a prayer practice, I can give praise and thanks and really mean it. I'm thankful for that because I don't want to take things for granted like I used to do."

I'm alive with spirit.

She continued, "I said to a friend recently, 'You are the person I can trust with my most intimate feelings. You listen and don't judge.' My friend was quiet for a minute and said the nicest thing anyone has ever said to me, 'Just to be in your presence is nurturing.' I never forgot that and as I struggle to be my best self in spite of some pain every day I feel appreciated as a person." I write:

> *Thank you, spirit, for my friend. Thank you for helping me feel love that's offered.*

In prayers of wonder we have a chance to better learn to give praise and say thank you. We can sit in appreciation at times when life blesses us with her beauty and grace. We can feel the feeling of praise and gratitude. We can say any number of things in prayers of wonder.

> *Beauty all around.*
> *Season, each lovely.*
> *My heart, people in my life.*
> *Thanks and praise, life as it is.*

As I give thanks, I think of all the people who have crossed my path to enrich my life: teachers who taught me valuable skills, my sister who was the constant companion of my youth, my son who by trusting me helped me find my most compassionate self, my partner who taught me that I can be loved as I am.

My students and clients show me that love heals and change does happen.

Many helped in ways I needed but could not see. Thank you.

I once wove baskets that looked like birds' nests and hung these pockets of beauty from small nails on the wall. Inside I'd write what I was thankful for that day, perhaps:

Thank you for the new growth outside my window.

The next day it might be another prayer.

Thank you for high boots and warm feet.

Practice: Create a Gratitude Prayer

Make a list of things for which you are grateful. Turn the list into a prayer and put it next to your bed. Just before sleep each night, say your gratitude prayer.

Through our prayers of gratitude, we come to notice and appreciate the things we might otherwise take for granted. We give thanks for small things in our lives that give us comfort: the heat, the blankets, the water, the bowl. We remember that blessings are warmth, nourishment, and shelter.

> ## Practice: The Meaning in Things
> Look around you right now. Name three things in your environment and their meaning to your prayer life, i.e., the clock of time means I have life to live, the candle calls me inward, the lamp illuminates that which I otherwise could not see.

I taught a workshop recently at a local church on writing for the spirit. The room was warm from the heat of the fireplace and I could sense we all felt close to each other in spirit. Just as we were closing, a woman asked for a final gift of things about which she might wonder and pray. Together the group spoke our prayers into the room.

Why am I here?
What is my ground?
Where is my spirit body?
Why must I pray?
What are some things that stay?
Do I listen to the song or the singer?
Why are we gathered here?
What is my heartbeat?
What can silence give me?
Why is nothing a good thing?
Where is death?
Why should I wish for a string of pearls?
Why does the abyss gaze at me?
How can I repack my old trunk?
What is it I don't know I love so much?

What way do I find shelter?
How can I reach the place I can't find?
How can I help the core of the apple earth?

Practice: Write a Prayer

About what would you like to wonder and pray? Write
a prayer.

In prayers of wonder we can question. We can sit in the delicious twilight of the day, watching the light and listening for answers. In prayers of thanks, we praise life as it is.

⚜

CHAPTER 2

Praying to the Part of Us That Is Spirit

We do not live chartless; we live in the wave of the spirit.

Webster's New World Dictionary defines prayer as "the act or practice of praying, to beg, to implore or beseech, implore, to ask earnestly; make supplication as to a deity; to God, a god, as by reciting certain set formulas." I propose that we expand the definition of prayer to include praying to our spirit as a source of life energy.

We don't need to *worship* spirit, nor give reverence to a deity. We can choose to hold our spirit as a partner in our life. Without a set formula for prayer, we can draw from many sources – our thoughts, feelings, and the world:

I pray to my spirit; kind, loving all life.

Our prayers of wonder allow us to feel our spirit in the mend of daily life, not to hold it up for exaltation. We want the feeling of spirit present in the everyday and that means not holding up spirit as something above us but seeing it as a part of who we are.

Being Equal to the Energy to Which We Pray

One of my friends tells me she doesn't adore or idealize the spirit energy to whom she prays each day because she wants a grassroots spirit, hearty, and vigorous. It was this spirit who guided her to retire at fifty-five with little money and much good health and energy. She says, "I prefer to be equal to the spirit that offers me guidance and the courage to take chances. We're in this together. I do my best to listen and follow. If the spirit wasn't at my side as a constant companion, I wouldn't have the confidence to take this time for myself."

Prayers of wonder do not have to bow us down to the spirit or our God but rather allow us to live with the knowledge that we have the song of holding within us and are a part of what we pray. We are both the vehicle for prayer and the prayer for which we ask. They remind us that we contain within us our spirit alive:

The spirit flows through me and is me.

When we do not worship, we are everything. We can use prayers of wonder as reminders that we are part of the problem and the solution. We can pray with wonder to rid ourselves of feelings of otherness and fear of difference. We can pray with the knowledge that we are all things including the evil doings of others:

All things, me. Light and goodness, be.

Use prayers of wonder to ground you in a desire to ease your wanting to be the best, knowing that the need to feel special separates us and that we can honor our gifts without being precious. Use prayers of wonder to express that you are concerned with self without being self-absorbed.

One of the central tenets of Goddess spirituality is "Know thyself." That is the principle we are after in our prayers of wonder.

Practice: Becoming a Part of Nature
Focus on a leaf or a flower in front of you and see how your prayer time can help you feel a part of nature.

Resisting the Need to Be Spectacular

Henri Nouwen, a tireless advocate of common prayer, writes in his article "Temptation" in *Sojourners* magazine that we must resist the temptation to be spectacular. "If you and I were to become known as relevant and powerful people, we would find ourselves burdened by the responsibilities that come with the image. If you make bread you have to deal with the hungry, and if you become king you have the headaches that come with governing. This is, perhaps, the temptation to be charismatic, to inspire the sort of awe in people that leaves your ego continually inflated but that lacks the obligations that might pull you back to earth."

The Quaker minister and educator Parker Palmer, in his book, *The Active Life*, talks of how wanting to be spectacular can lead us astray from the consideration that we are all one, "Every day we witness the pain of people who need to pray out, 'Look! I am here. I have power! I count!' That cry comes in many forms, some of them pathological – the loner who guns down innocents on a school playground to make a mark, the person who attempts suicide to get attention, people who live self-destructive lifestyles to get themselves known." (I would add the politician who thinks he knows a better way to do things even if it harms human rights and the earth's body.)

Many of us choose to live a cooperative life. We can use prayer to ground ourselves by sitting quietly and allowing ourselves to envision the beauty of the world that is given us. As we visualize quiet places we find the quiet place in ourselves to match. I use a prayer of the spirit earth to bring me to deeper truths:

Hills and valleys, let me touch the ground.

I find my worn copy of Rilke's *Letters to A Young Poet* and read: "And if there is one more thing that I must say to you, it is this: Don't think that the person who is trying to comfort you now lives untroubled among the simple and quiet words that sometimes give you pleasure. His life has much trouble and sadness, and remains far behind yours. If it were otherwise, he would never have been able to find those words."

Setting ourselves above others is hurtful to our souls because it slows down our search for deep identity. It is hurtful to others because they must find ways to detach when they are around your toxic energy and still feel good about themselves. As we strive to be part of the healing of the world, to be a prayer in others' lives and to do nothing that would hurt their spirit, we can turn to prayer for help. As we examine our behaviors, we can pray to be the compassionate force in the room of people, ever using our self-examination of the in breath and our relationship to others as the out breath of peace.

Practice: Equal in Spirit
See yourself holding hands with a circle of people. See how the ancient form of the circle makes each of us equal. Imagine your friends in a circle holding hands with you. Your co-workers. Your neighbors. See how you are all equal in spirit.

The In Breath and the Out Breath

In Gail Straub's book *The Rhythm of Compassion*, she writes: "Without the in breath of self-care and reflection we can't sustain our involvement with the suffering of the world, nor do we have the clarity of heart required for the complex challenges we face. On the other hand, without the out breath of compassionate engagement with society, our inner work implodes upon itself, leading to the dead end of narcissism and spiritual emptiness. To sustain life on all levels we need to breathe in *and* we need to breathe out."

It is with this awareness of the interrelatedness of ourselves, others, and our planet that we become the prayer we seek. We live with our arms wrapped around others and the planet, our hands placed gently on our heart.

Practice: In Breath, Out Breath
Noticing your breath say, *I am all things* with the in breath. Say, *I am connected* with the out breath.

Accessing Spirit

૪

I recently had an experience with a form of prayer new to me that I think of as a way of praying with wonder: a labyrinth walk. The labyrinth is an ancient mystical tool, a sacred pattern carved out on the ground that is then walked in meditation. Labyrinths are found in many cultures all over the world.

Because there is only one way in and one way out (no blind alleys or dead ends, as in a maze), walking a labyrinth helps us find our own center. Once you start on the path you find yourself shifting into an easier, more blessed place as you twist and turn to the heart of the labyrinth, the center, the place of wholeness and unity. Labyrinths remind us that there is no trick to spirituality. Everybody wins, all connected.

I entered the labyrinth at Grace Cathedral in San Francisco with a group of women I didn't know and with whom I seemingly had little in common. The cathedral was hushed except for the sounds coming from a harp. I became absorbed in the walking, I felt my breath. I passed a few women and a few passed me. I looked back and one woman seemed to be dancing. Ahead, in the center, someone was sitting in prayer. I looked up and a woman in her seventies gave me the smile of an angel. I was *home* with the walk and the women and the spirit.

I realized that the labyrinth is a metaphor for life. All we need to do is get on the path of prayer. The path will have its delays and turns, it may move into a direction we hadn't thought to go. But all we have to do is follow the path and we will better reach the spirit.

Practice: Prayer in Every Step

Find a labyrinth in your town or a lovely place to take a walk. Walk very slowly focusing on your step saying:

Every step I take is on the path of prayer.

By developing this wise spirit voice inside of us through prayer we are breaking new ground. We are developing trust in that voice, and at the same time praying to an energy that is equal to us. As we pray, we find we want to pray. We like the feeling. We like the intent to connect with the spirit of things. We like the fact that prayer takes a bit of quiet noticing and a bit of solitude to reflect and listen. We offer ourselves time to be in prayer and pretty soon we find that without prayer something is missing for us because prayer allows us to find the depth of meaning in our everyday.

✣

CHAPTER 3

Praying in Focused Attention

As a bud is to a blossom, prayer is to the spirit.

The form of prayer most of us know best is sitting quietly with our hands folded, our eyes closed talking to our spirit. This is a beautiful way to pray, our minds and bodies totally focused. I can sit like this and feel my concentration deepen by repeating my prayer or by using a bit of time to allow mind and body to settle down. After awhile I can tell I am in prayer; my everyday mind allows the spirit room to move me.

Perhaps you remember a time in your life when you were singing and you were song. Or, as you danced, you were music. That is a form of prayer because you are one with your spirit as you express and create. This feeling of oneness is the unmixed attention needed for prayer. "Absolute, unmixed attention." That's what Sophie Burnham calls prayer in *A Book of Angels*.

I'll never forget a time when I was in prayer with my "unmixed attention" on creating beauty. I was drawing a chalk mural on the blackboard at school, and I had the feeling of being a part of the color of things and "I" disappeared. I was cobalt blue in all its brilliance. The teacher softly called my

name, startling me. I was surprised to be at school with children all around. In that moment I was more than half in
heaven, alive and connected with beauty and creation.

Anything we do can be done slowly and can help us better
feel at one with the activity as part of our personal prayer. In
Buddhism we hear of walking meditation where you are one
with your body as you walk and experience the moment. Or
eating, one raisin at a time, as a meditation which allows us to
really notice and be in the moment.

In self-hypnosis, which is used in psychology as a relaxation
tool for anxiety, we are asked to follow our breath. We close our
eyes and envision and practice breathing a belly breath, as if we
could breathe right into our belly. We know we have taken the
deepest breath possible if we feel the abdomen move in and
out. We stay with the breath, in and out, in this way, visualize
a special place with all its beauty, the sounds, any gentle
movements, fragrances, anything you might want to touch.

We find ourselves in a place of beauty for our ease and relax
there awhile. We enjoy this place and the calm it brings us
makes us feel whole. We use this state to work therapeutically
but it is also a prayer of wonder:

I am spirit.

This is not unlike the meditation that many of us have studied.
We find the single point attention of the breath or the candle
flame. We find peace by living with the focus and let thoughts
pass through; the focus on the breath. This is the readiness
for prayer, the place where the spirit exists – and an openness
to spirit.

The prayer we are talking about here is different from meditation, however. In meditation we clear our energy to single-minded focus and look for the answers from within our "Buddha" nature. In prayer we rely on the "Buddha" nature within and without knowing that answers may also come from an external voice or energy: the spirit power, the meaning of nature, the energy that flowers in all things.

It doesn't matter whether we pray, meditate, or use self-hypnosis; all are useful spiritual methods. There are many ways to open our hearts and focus our attention.

Practice: Contemplative Prayer

Find a place where you can sit quietly in wonder and just follow your breath. When you feel a calming, choose a word or phrase that has some spiritual significance for you and repeat it – Mary, god, spirit, love, and peace, peace begins with me, here I am, love, harmony. Feel the sound of your voice in your body. Notice how you become what you are chanting.

Practice: Ask Your Heart to Open

Sit and breathe and follow the breath into the belly with your mind's eye. Feel your abdomen go in and out. Do this ten times until you can tell your breath is a belly breath.

Now imagine your heart as a lovely lotus flower, white with twelve shiny petals. Gently watch in your mind's eye as one by one the petals open. Count them as they open – one to twelve – and with each number see and feel the petal open and your heart open. When you reach twelve, notice that the flower has opened fully and that coming from the center is a golden light.

This is love energy; feel it stream out and surround you. Side to side, the top of your head, to your feet, you feel surrounded with a gentle golden light of love energy.

Now feel this energy reach out into the room. Imagine now the room full of golden light, love energy, spirit energy, and feel it reach out into the world and fill the air with a soft golden light. The light spreads and touches all things – people, plants, animals, the oceans, and countries of the world. You are all things. Your heart is open and you belong to the world in love. You are love and in love with all things.

Bring into this prayerful meditation, the chant:

I am the light. I am the light. I belong to the world in love.

As we turn to prayer, we see the spirit in all things. "All the way to heaven is heaven," said St Catherine of Siena. Spirituality has no walls; it belongs to daily life. Much as we eat our oatmeal and make our beds, we can bring prayer to the daily mixtures of our life:

Prayers of wonder, everywhere.

When I want to focus, I call to mind the sun on my back in my garden. I remember a peaceful place on a favorite beach where the sand stretches on and on, a place big and grand enough to take all my vision.

As far as the eye can see,
the creation of sand and its forms
meeting the ebb and flowing sea.
I belong here.
I am part of this.

Other times I can't visualize without sitting quietly and breathing deeply. I might think about the flowing river. If the current is too strong, I'll move downstream until I can feel comfortable entering the water to swim or drift with it. Soon the act of swimming or drifting and the calm water allows me to feel transformed to a peaceful place of unmixed attention.

Sometimes, I write in my journal until I reach that focused place of balance. What is important is our intent to pray; that intent *will lead us to* prayer. Prayer can be an intention to reach out for offerings of our good energy and wishes or for self-healing.

Just use your breath, concentrate on a candle flame, a mantra, a feeling, a vision of oneness to calm you. Sit quietly and center. Tenderly hush the voice that asks if you are doing it right. Try to ease your nagging worry. All that matters is that you intend to pray and bring prayer to your heart. Just to want to pray prayers of wonder allows you to feel the gratitude for what you can do.

CHAPTER 4

❧

Coming Into the Present

I am alive with feeling.
I bless my body.

Any experience in life can be a prayer; all you need is an awareness that you are right where you are. Simply to be present is to
be in prayer. To smell the rich smell of coffee, the grass after a
rain. To see the beauty of the rock garden and the wing and song
of the jay reminds us that we have a part of flying and song. To
taste basil and parsley from our garden and add fresh tomatoes
and pine nuts allows prayer to be in our mouths as a blessing.

You can have the spirit with you in the shower as you lather
yourself with soap, feeling the hot steamy water and the rough
washcloth, smooth soap.

Practice: The Soulful Shower
Take a soulful shower and note how your body holds your
aliveness and spirit. Change the water temperature to
very cold if you'd like to really come alive in the moment!

When You Just Can't Get There

Sometimes, however, no matter what we do we feel over-whelmed and can't stay in the here and now. We know we're not in touch with our bodies, but so it is. Just yesterday I suggested to Joe, a client with a high level of anxiety, that he use physical exercise as his prayer for now. I explained that exercise is often the step before a prayer practice. It helps the mind single focus, whether pumping iron or getting the ball into the hole or through the hoop. I am confident that once Joe has come back to his spirit through his body, he will feel less overwhelmed and more likely to be able to single focus on prayer:

As I feel my body, I feel my spirit.

Practice: Counting Nouns

When you feel overwhelmed and have a sense you're not in your body take a walk and count nouns. Sturdy things: shoes, boardwalk, tree, wall, brick, house. Stay away from adjectives until a day of feeling sad: magic, gorgeous, warm. Walk naming the nouns around you over and over until you find yourself here and now in your yellow jacket on this day of wonder.

We live to experience life. Author and lecturer Joseph Campbell tells us to "put our heads in the mouth of the lion." We pray to live and feel our spirits in today. It is what is given to us if we can but notice that there is marvel in the sky and clouds, the fresh air, even the cold breeze that brings the snow.

Here it is. Life and spirit, our daily bread.

Becoming Aware

If we don't want to live disassociated, distracted lives, we can use prayer to ground ourselves in this experience we are having of life. We can pray to keep ourselves from becoming numb, to say that we know there is something more than the material things we collect and covet – and that is the human spirit and the soul of things.

Thank you for this day, the loving people in my life, the bird outside my window.

Several of my clients these days have dealt well with the external world of work and money. Keeping busy and productive makes them happy. I find their energy "bright-eyed" and attractive. They are upbeat go-getters and I can feel the strength in their willingness to set a goal and achieve it. However, they want to feel more. One man lost both his parents in a six-month period and suddenly realized how important family was to him. He realized that his wife and kids no longer bothered to include him in family decisions because he just wasn't around much. He had been content to be the major breadwinner and to be left alone to his reading and sports the rest of the time. That is no longer enough.

Another man, a scientist, realized he had been in the world of the mind and wanted more connection. Others aren't drawn to him because he isn't feeling; he relies on facts. He wants to feel looser and freer with others and wonders if it's possible to have a spouse. It took quite a lot to get his attention – anxiety attacks after meeting a nice woman – to realize he really knew nothing of being equal to another, so used was he to being the boss at work and alone at home.

I ask them to tell me their life stories. I am interested in the plot of it, of course, and what they choose to relate as important and what they leave out. I am more interested in the feelings that go with the plot. We take our time. We explore what the feelings might have been. We sit together and imagine how it would be to have felt that. I often ask them to start a journal.

We use different techniques to recover feelings: talk, breath work, hypnotherapy, writing. In time, just being in these processes and feeling safe with a witness, the feelings come, and they show that they are human to themselves and each other. I also have found it helpful to have them do some of the feeling work in front of their partners; this makes them sympathetic friends and helps with situations that might have once been adversarial.

Slowly they awaken.

To pray the longings of your heart is to be heard by the strongest energy of life, the spirit energy, and in the spirit energy, you find meaning and joy in the everyday.

As I touch, let me be touched.

Another client worries about the nature of her prayers. She is a junior high school English teacher and enjoys her work. She has a loving husband who grades her spelling papers on Thursday nights. She is afraid her prayers for a child of her own are selfish when there are so many children who need help. We talk awhile, pray together:

> *Praise to the child that may someday come through me.*
> *Praise to my husband and all things gentle.*

I find that those who worry whether their prayers are "selfish" are usually the least selfish of all; just the question shows that they are aware of self in relationship. I'm thinking of a time when a young man was totally vulnerable with me and asked if I thought he knew how to love. Soulful, he need have had no worry about being good to the people in his life.

We can use our prayers to praise what we are and not what we *want*. If we want to be part of the good of our times *and* to nurture ourselves, personal prayer can help us find the balance.

> *I am a person of worth.*
> *I find the balance.*
> *I see the glory in the world as it is and I am part of that glory.*

Whatever is in the human heart is a human thing for which to pray.

I am all things.
I pray for all things.
One spirit, one life,
goodness abounds.

I have a cousin who just learned she will be a new grandma. She was delighted to hear the news but also felt a wave of grief, which shocked her. She was afraid that her son would judge her harshly as a grandmother, much as he had her skills as a mother. "Another grief," fear said. She continued to pray and realized that she would never be the mother he wanted or the grandma he wanted. That was his grief and his idea of how sacrificing a woman should be.

She realized that she could be just who she is. Yes, she would have to work through her sadness and anger at feeling unfairly judged while listening to what he had to say. She could say she was sorry when appropriate. She could pray to be released from hurtful feelings.

I did my best and sometimes it wasn't good enough. I'm sorry.
I offer possibilities. I offer praise for possibilities of healing our sorrows, and living our lives.

This Is Who I Am

⚜

The days of the "self-made man" are over in our country. That reality really only worked for a very few and has become an American myth. We know that many an intelligent and hard-working man and woman did not fail but rather the system of competition and greed failed them if they had a family of children to raise and chose to be attentive to their little ones and wouldn't put in long hours that success demanded. Or perhaps we weren't that personable or lucky. Some of us are average. Others have too much to overcome from our childhood situation to really be able to focus on a career. We may be part of a group who is discriminated against and cannot find our way around the stones in the road.

As it is, I am content. As it could be, I vision and work.

We may not have the stomach for business or its politics or we may choose to go into a helping profession that pays little because it is valued less. We may work in business but choose to work at a low management level where the responsibility leaves time for family commitments or creative work. We may choose to work in a nontoxic business environment where workers meet goals in ways that make everyone feel good about their efforts and values, forgoing high market salary. We may work for ourselves and conduct business in an ethical way, succeed to meet our bills and prepare for the future, yet find the years are not getting easier in terms of finding business or finances.

We have learned in the last decades that we indeed need each other and that that is a good thing. We help each other in our families, friendships, and communities. We try to be the fair and kind person at work. We bring prayer to work in our briefcase and heart. We remember to give praise for all we have been given.

I praise the hand that holds me.

CHAPTER 5

Offering Ourselves to Prayer

My life of hardship and taffy, I offer.

One of my writing students has never believed in church or prayer or religion. She was hurt by the church in her youth and doesn't believe in a higher power. She is a wonderful, nurturing person who believes in the goodness of people. She found herself, in her fifties, not only with a failed business in the dot com economy and the need to find another job or a new way to make a living, but a sudden ending to a relationship as well.

She knew that it was the economy that killed her business and that she wasn't alone in this. She knew that if she had only listened to her partner's history she would have realized that this person didn't stick around through hard times. She could have felt terrible about herself or felt defeated but instead she chose to experiment with prayer.

She had rarely prayed because she had always felt that prayer was a way people soothed themselves by asking something of a God who wasn't listening anyway. But then she began to wonder why soothing couldn't be okay and why she shouldn't get help back when she had been there for so many.

She felt a bit of a failure and for the first time in her life she couldn't shake feeling down. We talked about her situation and gradually she let her friends know the hard time she was having.

Instead of giving up and feeling defeated, she gave up in a turning-it-over kind of way, where she was admitting she didn't have all the answers. She remembers wringing her hands but feeling lighter. It was as if all her burdens were lifted.

Practice: Lead Me

Offer this prayer of surrender:

Here I am. Hands up. Lead me.

She said she began to sleep and eat well, and did her best to look for work although it was difficult. She accepted her friends' offer of soup and movies. She continued therapy and accepted sliding scale rate. She started to list in a journal the good things she did for herself.

> *Thank you for long nights of sleep and healthy eating, a walk and a swim.*

As the days and weeks went by, she felt herself held in the hands of light. She couldn't explain it. She said, "I just believed somehow I would be helped. That something worthwhile would happen."

As it turned out, a former customer had an opening in her company and offered the position to Katha. The pay was good and she knew she would enjoy the work. She realized she'd be glad to get out of the limelight of marketing for awhile. Sometimes our prayers are answered in the most unexpected ways.

> *Thank you for the change I needed.*

All through these days and months of change, she took the time to notice every turn of corner that was bettering her life. She'd sit and notice and be silent. She sometimes found herself saying words of gratitude:

> *Thank you. The world is good. People are good. Good things happen to me. I give and receive help.*

When I told her I was writing a book on prayer, she said she didn't believe in God but she had this story to tell. She said that if I used her story in my book I should be sure to say she still doesn't know what to think but she will never forget that feeling of not being so in control, so in charge, and letting spirit help her.

> *I am puzzled by, but praise, the letting go.*

Even if we do not feel the spirit's presence, it doesn't mean that the spirit is absent. I have found that if we continue to pray, the "quiet time" is often a time before growth. On days when we feel empty and there is no presence to be felt, just offer yourself to prayer and be there.

Practice: Sitting in the Silence

Sit quietly and discover for yourself the different ways you are in the silence.

I remember a time I had gotten myself into a particularly confusing situation. I prayed but I was quite nervous and didn't know what I needed to do. I was hurt and confused. I talked to my friends. I continued to pray and didn't feel connected as my nervousness caused a distancing from myself. After a week or so, I remembered to stop figuring it out and offer myself in prayer. I did so and soon my direction became clear; I was startled to see how obvious the solution was.

Letting prayers find their own way reminds me of a book, *Adventures in Prayer* by Catherine Marshall, in which she writes, "I believe the old cliché, 'God helps those who help themselves,' is not only misleading but dead wrong. My most spectacular answers to prayer have come when I was so helpless, so out of control as to be able to do nothing at all for myself."

I thought of how I too had found a new way to pray in troubled times, the God of my childhood living dormant in me. But I thought of how prayer doesn't care whether we have a church or a god. Prayer wants nothing of us but our heart and, if our heart is confused, we can offer our body; we can sit quietly and face the light of prayer.

When hope is dim and the world has gone mad, we can bring prayer into our world. I watched the invasion of Iraq, a "war" conducted in our name, and was horrified as I heard a Philippine mother watch her POW son on the Al Jazeera network quake in fear in the hands of his captor. I think: "No mother should ever have to have this happen to her; her face in the papers, a collapsed mountain of pain." I felt so helpless and found myself praying for all the mothers of soldiers doing what they think is best. I hate war and pray for the men who wage war for any reason.

We humans, find peace within, and grow a world of peace without.

The Many Paths of Prayers

❧

Sometimes we have regrets on how we've not brought prayer into our lives and the lives of loved ones. When my son said he wished he had had a more religious upbringing, I realized I didn't talk much about my spiritual beliefs because I was brought up to keep politics and religion to myself. I hadn't talked to my son much about a spirit energy because I was unsure. I didn't take him to churches much because it made a difference to me not to be treated equally as a woman in the eyes of the Church and now I felt I had shortchanged him.

Thank you for helping me find my prayer.
Thank you for the imagination and searching of my son.

In thinking about this, I realized God for me was a kindly being but it was a spirit source that seemed all around me – about the earth and in friendships and in my heart. I had brought prayer into my life through a connection to the earth and woman friends. I had brought prayer into my life through compassion and love, not God.

Thank you for friendship: seed, blossom, and berry.

I had to hope that my encouragement of my son's travels around the world had been a soulful thing. To listen to his backpacking over mountains and sleeping in valleys, I had to trust that the spirit of the earth was in him. I remembered him telling me long distance from Thailand that we were watching the same stars. He seemed a soulful man and I hoped that the spirit of the earth could bring him what he needed and I encouraged him to talk about his beliefs if he was interested. He is a child of the spirit.

Practice: Connecting with a Friend Through Prayer

Ask someone to pray while watching the same stars as you, and feel the spiritual connection between yourself and your friend.

My friend Carol said that her prayers to Mary or Jesus were seen to her as praying to those who had the pathway to God since Mary and Jesus were sent to us as holy people. She was content to pray to them because of her belief. She brought prayer into her life from her upbringing of love for and from the Church. However, it made sense to her that others who had not had the same kind parish priest or her family, where religion was used as a positive energy, would need to find another way to connect to religion or spirituality.

A journey, each of us, a way.

I marveled that she could both believe in a Christian God and yet see another's point of view and need to believe in something different. What she believed enlivened her life and she offered others true religious freedom to believe or not believe. She demonstrates by the way she thinks and lives her life that there is no need of violence over differences.

A student of mine decided that sin and Church and their attitudes toward gays were hurting him. He could no longer pretend to be anything other than himself, even though the minister had said it was not a sin as long as he wasn't *acting on* his homosexuality. He decided to leave the Church and continue on in his loving relationship of thirteen years. He moved in with his partner and made their relationship even more of a "family," yet he missed the prayers and communion with God. He knew God loved him as he was and, after several years of floundering with belief and loneliness, he uses personal prayer to connect himself to spirit:

I feel the good of all sentient beings.

To allow himself community around the sounds of music he loves, he has joined the San Francisco Gay Men's Chorus. Nowadays he is bringing prayer into his life through song:

Thank you for the song in my heart.

PART TWO

Prayers of Possibility

Let me wander in holy groves among sacred trees –
peace in the heart of the day.

We often turn to prayer when we need help with
something that is happening in our life. We're not
necessarily asking of some force out there, we just
turn to prayer to help us get quiet enough to hear
our own spirit's answer:

Quiet, let me find myself.

At other times we pray in the ongoing struggle and joy to be more humane and alive. We pray for ourselves, we pray with a broken heart in our hands like the bird with a broken wing. We ask to be heard and not be alone. We ask to be cupped in the hands of some great energy.

We pray for others that they might thrive and heal. We turn to the spirit with our longings and ask that the spirit help us all find forgiveness so we will not be separated. We ask that our country, our earth, and all sentient beings be included in our love and protected by our spiritual longing.

CHAPTER 6

୵

Asking for Help

Steady path, steady footstep.

To live a full, rich, balanced life, we sometimes need to ask for help. It's only natural. So many of us were shamed at some point along the way about having needs. We forget that we were once tiny little bundles that did not know how to eat solid foods or talk or walk. Being sometimes helpless is the natural state of things, but we learned to fear our helplessness. Now we need to relearn to honor dependence and to know that independence is taught gradually and can even be something of an illusion.

What we are is interdependent – we need others. And so we might pray:

Loved in my need, blessed be.

Sometimes a student or client will tell me that they don't like to pray. They say it makes them feel as if they are not being independent. They feel they are looking for an easy way out. As I examine their lives with them, I see that these same people are often the ones who had the toughest road to travel. Hardships with no support. Early messages that told them it was somehow dangerous to show their needs, that they should never disclose that they don't know how to do something or that they need help, that they should always hide their needs for emotional support.

I tell them that reaching out to me is a big step in the right direction. I suggest that if they can trust me to help and not shame them, maybe they can also trust the spirit within them. Just maybe there is a life-long sense of inner support that is waiting for their acknowledgement. I ask them to do what they always do but notice from time to time that a spirit is sitting in their heart loving them. And I let time go by, time to notice the truth that they are held by love.

Sitting in the heart of spirit.

I don't know about you but it helps me to think that my spirit is routing for me. It makes me feel less alone. Sometimes I like to think of my spirit as a pair of sturdy brown oxfords. I know I'll do the "hard" things but want spirit's steady footstep as I do.

When we ask spirit for help through prayer, we do it not in the expectation that prayer will do for us what we can do for ourselves. We push the plow and plant the crops; we row the boat toward shore. We do what we can and are happy to be able to push through our fears and use our strengths and skills. We ask in the confidence that we do our best and could use a helping hand from time to time.

Lend me a bough for help.

Practice: Learning Through the Difficult Times
Write down four difficult times in your life and what you
learned from going through these times. Make a prayer
out of what you learned such as:

*I ask for help developing patience and trusting that
in time I will see what's right for me. I know when to
hold on; I know when to let go. Please help me trust
that you are with me, spirit.*

We pray to let go of past hurts, to let the past be what it is: over,
gone, done. We pray knowing that our happiness depends on
living in the present with the past released into the river of
time. We read and know we should do this but still we don't
know how. And so we pray for guidance.

Guide my path.

We pray in the realization that if we knew what to do we would
probably have done it by now, and allow prayer to lead the way.
In this way, we learn patience. We don't always get what we
want when we want it. Life doesn't work that way. Instead, we
pray for the awareness to know how to release the past, how to
be in the present:

Time and prayer on my side.
Spirit, guide me to what I need to learn.

As we face life's fear, we work on our own gratitude and generosity. We deal with the difficult while increasing our positive thoughts and connections right at the point of our pain.

We are our fear and more than our fear. We give our thanks and gifts to the world.

In repeating this prayer, in the face of fear, we seek and give love. As we explore fear, we allow it to dissolve into places of love in our life until we see life as love.

My mind filled with love
for flecks of dust
a tiny shell,
grey feathers,
the wind, the ocean, the bird in flight.

Sometimes we can find a traditional source that speaks to our need, our longing. This Celtic blessing is such a prayer for me.

May the blessing of light be on you – light without and light within. May the blessed sunlight shine on you and warm your heart till it glows like a great peat fire.

or, the old Irish prayer:

May your day be touched by a bit of Irish luck, brightened by a song in your heart, and warmed by the smiles of the people you love.

In Alice Walker's *The Color Purple*, we are reminded that: "God ain't he or she, but it … don't look like anything. It ain't something you can look at apart from anything else, including you. I believe God is everything. Everything that is or ever was or ever will be. And when you can feel that, and be happy to feel that, you've found it."

Prayers That Stream Out of Our Hearts

Often we find that a prayer from our heart is the most immediate prayer. The source doesn't matter and can come from many places in your life: a movie, a book you're reading, a poem. As Walker says, "God is everything." I would add you can find the spirit *in* everything.

> *I hear you at the corner store,*
> *see you in the glow of light in a painting of the forest,*
> *touch you on my child's shoulder.*
> *Everywhere, spirit. I long for your presence.*
> *It is given.*

A client recently told me, "Many times I have found life to be difficult and I wasn't sure I could manage all that was asked of me. Years of being cast in a role as a wife and mother, when I could not find myself outside of those roles; years of single parenting and the hardships of little time or money made me search for something to sustain me. Addictions didn't work; I was much too responsible to not meet my obligations fully.

"I found deep friendships and solace in the changing form of my relationship with my ex-husband. Most of all, I saw the light in my little girls' eyes and knew I was capable of love. I found myself turning to a spirit I knew little of, asking for guidance.

Help me.

"Without realizing it, prayer was waiting in my body. It seems like once I could rely on friends, I could ask for help from my spirit. That doesn't really make sense unless others came to me as spirit and my trust enlarged. Whatever it was, I no longer have the feeling of being alone and I am most certainly myself now, for better or worse, I am responsible for my life with the help of my spirit."

> *Guided to your care.*
> *It is given.*

Often, prayers are found in the voice of our spirit who knows us well. We may be walking to our office after parking our car and sense spring in the air and find ourselves connecting to our spiritual self in prayer: Let a soft breeze come to me. Or, we may be upset with a parent and need some solace that things will get easier as time goes by:

> *Let time be my friend.*
> *Help us heal.*

We may find that using writing as a form of prayer is a way to get to prayer of unmixed attention and deep focus.

Practice: Writing as Prayer

Pulitzer prize-winning poet William Stafford once asked us to follow the golden thread. Just let the spool of thread be thrown out before you and follow the thread with your words. You don't have to know where you are going with your words or how it will end. Just start and follow the golden thread. Your thought will take care of itself, often revealing a connection to spirit.

Practice: Streaming

Try the streaming method, in which you write without stopping until you feel finished and just allow whatever surfaces to be placed on the page. The streaming method is good practice in surrendering and letting go of outcome and often helps you find the single-minded focus necessary for prayer.

Don't expect perfection. Let your intent to connect with yourself and spirit be the prayer. Just because you didn't feel it, doesn't mean your spirit isn't surrounding you and holding you in its ample lap. This is where faith kicks in and you can trust that like the changing of the shadow to the light, in time you will feel the truth of your connection.

We might turn to prayer in writing when we become aware that we are having judgmental thoughts – and we all do. My client Joseph held onto his resentment of a past girlfriend for ten years. Yes, he had been treated badly and was betrayed. However, he came to see that by being in a difficult relationship he didn't have to look at his own intimacy problems and this was quite a shock to him.

> *Layers of myself,*
> *revealed.*

It was when he entered into a new relationship with a kind person that he finally realized he had trouble with closeness. He saw that in a kind, intimate relationship, he felt over-whelmed, and feelings of too much expectation from his child-hood made him feel almost asthmatic. Being in a difficult relationship with all its comings and goings had masked his fear of intimacy.

As he grew in awareness of himself, Joseph continued to journal and pray and was able to talk to his new love. They worked it out so he could have the space needed and she could be assured that he would let her know when he needed that space before he became irritated.

Joseph's first prayer of his life came out of an appreciation of what intimacy really meant and how exciting it was to know and be himself. He found that he loved his girlfriend more, the more he could be his true self with her.

> *Blessed be, you and me.*

The prayers of the heart bring the longing that you will create a new history of love for yourself and bring prayer back into the centerfold of your life. With that choice, you will be walking in the sun with your spiritual self, moving away from any harried and angry place. Spirit, me.

We long to love and know that one way of loving ourselves and others is in self-less prayer. We learn love and give love by offering ourselves to the energy of the world. We might pray:

Let me be a vehicle for positive change.

We pray and persist. We don't lose heart and we ask with intensity and hope. By asking we are in the state of engagement that is life-giving in itself. Hope is the attitude that helps faith and we rely on prayer to give us faith. We begin to live in spiritual circles where to pray heals us and prayer itself creates the state of healing.

Prayer has helped me clarify what I believe in. I was surprised to discover through prayer that I believe in a personal spirit and god energy. Of course, even with a personal spirit difficulties do occasionally come my way, but my spirit helps me deal with what comes and continue on with good heart.

Good heart, carry on.

In *The Essential Gandhi*, Louis Fischer writes that Gandhi was pleading the cause of independence for India at a prayer meeting aboard a ship bound for London in 1931 when he felt that prayer saved his life.

"I had my share of public and private experiences that threw me into despair. If I was able to get out of that despair, it was because of prayer. It came out of sheer necessity. I found myself in a blight where I could not possibily be happy without it. And as time went on, my faith in God increased and more irresistible became the yearning for prayer. Life seemed to be dull and vacant without it. In spite of the despair staring me in the face on the political horizon, I have never lost my peace. That peace comes from prayer. I am indifferent as to the form. Everyone is a law unto himself in that respect. Let everyone try and find that as result of daily prayer, he adds something new to his life."

We, like Gandhi, may come to prayer from necessity, but as we pray we may find that we *want* to pray. Soon when we're not praying we'll feel that something is missing. Prayer allows us to find the depth of meaning in our everyday. It allows us to long and dream and ask for the good of ourselves and others.

Spirit, let me find you.

There was a time in my life when I was having trouble carrying a baby. I had had a miscarriage and then a stillborn before the birth of my premature son (who grew into a healthy child and is now a strapping young adult). There was really nothing anyone could say to me that could ease my pain although simple kindness helped. I found that the best retreat I could find was in the quiet of my soul; I needed prayer to hold me until I could find ease.

From that difficult time in my life, I always remember that I can go to the ocean for solace, and I do, or I can make sure I renew myself with my own resource of prayer and solitude.

When I hold more than my body can bear, I let go into the sea and become a bottle thrown, new wishes and hopes a'floating.

Practice: Renewing Your Spirit

Find a place in the world to which you can go for solace and renewal. Go there whenever you need to restore your sense of spirit.

✿

CHAPTER 7

Prayer Methods, Direct vs. Indirect

I am my best self in prayer.

Many clients tell me that they pray in a direct way, for a specific outcome, because they want to make sure they ask for the right thing. They are unsure of their needs much of the time and want to be sure that the spirit understands exactly what they're looking for. This is fine as long as you hold no illusion that you know best and as long as your intent isn't to control another through prayer. If it makes you feel better and you are clear about what you want, while doing no harm to others, then pray for exactly what you want.

I am clear.
I don't want to argue anymore.
Bring peace to my life.
Let me learn to talk differently,
allowing others to disagree
while I remain calm.

When I pray, I try to remember to visualize an open door at the end of my prayers. The open door to me is a symbol of the idea, *may the best happen*, meaning that I want the spirit to help create the best for all and if there's something I don't yet know or understand, I'll be open to it when the insight comes. I pray this way to make sure my wants are known even if I don't have the best picture yet. It's like a prayer-in-progress.

In indirect prayer, we acknowledge we do not know what is best. We do not have access to the whole picture and our prayers reflect that.

I sometimes pray in a direct way, for a specific outcome, but I would never do so for a friend who does not believe in prayer. That would be an invasion of their privacy; no one has the right to impose on anyone else their own sense of what's right. Most of these same friends say they don't mind an indirect prayer that just asks for their good, however. If I pray for them, I can ask directly for good and indirectly for what that good may be.

> *Spirit, give _____ what she needs to heal.*
> *Spirit, pay attention to _____.*

Here are some examples of direct and indirect prayer. As you explore your own prayer life, you will probably find a time and place for both.

> *Let _____ earn more money (direct)*
> *Let _____ prosper (indirect)*
>
> *Help me earn more money (direct)*
> *Help me feel secure (indirect)*

Let me travel to Greece (direct)
Fuel my imagination (indirect)

Heal my sore joints (direct)
Heal my body (indirect)

Watch over _____'s safe return (direct)
Keep _____ safe (indirect)

Practice: Direct Prayer
Say two direct prayers, repeating the prayers in your mind.

Practice: Indirect Prayer
Say two indirect prayers, repeating the prayers in your mind.

In southwest writer Peggy Pond Church's account of the Manhattan Project in her nonfiction, *House at Otowi Bridge: The Story of Edith Warner and Los Alamos,* she tells the story of Edith Warner, a woman instrumental in bridging the divide between the Los Alamos scientists of World War II and the peoples of the neighboring San Ildefonso pueblo, Church quotes Warner: "This morning I went to the river bank to pray. I knew then that the ancient ones were wise to pray for peace and beauty and not for specific gifts except fertility which is continued life. And I saw that if one has even a small degree of the ability to take into and unto himself the peace and beauty the gods surround him with, it is not necessary to ask for more."

Novelist, poet, and leading expert on mysticism Evelyn Underhill talks of the need for goals in prayers in her collected papers, "The life of prayer is so great and various there is something in it for everyone. It is like a garden which grows everything from alpines to potatoes."

Several years ago, a cousin of mine was dying and the doctors said there was nothing to be done. I didn't want to give her false hope by saying she would regain her good health; I didn't want to visit her pretending she was fine and offer some prayer to what we both knew was not true.

My cousin had been a role model to me when I was young. She lived in exotic California and I was a creative child in a small town in Ohio who dreamed of living in a large city full of the arts. Now I wanted to give her something. I knew that hope and prayer comforted people and that miracles do happen.

I hadn't solved the puzzle of what to do but as I walked into her room I saw her face light up and I knew she wanted me there. I went over to her bed with the books I had brought, placing my hand on hers. I pulled my chair closer, touched her forehead and then put my head in her lap for a moment. She petted me and laid back and relaxed.

After making her more comfortable, I read her part of a catalog of an art show I had recently seen. She listened with interest and gratitude. We talked about beauty and vulnerability, the rawness that touches on mortality. As she began to tire she reached out for my hand and we prayed.

We sat quietly awhile listening to the distant noises of the hospital and feeling our prayers. We had created love in prayers. She was wished safe passage. I'd be with her.

On my own, I simply prayed:

The spirit knows. Thy will be done.

We had a sweet month of visits before she passed away. I visited her with books and prayers. She accepted my visits as the gifts they were. I let her know how special she was to me.

I surprised myself by using *Thy will be done* in my prayer. Like so many people, I had always had a hard time with the whole concept of turning things over to God, as if we have no choice and don't need to take care of ourselves. But these days I have a different take on it. We are in charge of ourselves and our lives to the extent that we can do what seems best for ourselves and others. We are responsible for doing what it takes to make our own dreams come true. We can pray that we are on the right path and continue to do what needs to be done. If something is difficult for a period of time, we can ask our prayers to guide us:

God, Goddess, Spirit, guide me to your side.

But we also have to recognize that we are not in charge and that there's a big difference between taking charge of ourselves and our actions and being in charge. None of us is in charge of the universe and frankly it only seems as if we are in charge of ourselves.

What a great relief. All we have to do is take care of ourselves. The Goddess will handle the rest and if it's not according to the greater good, the project or dream will not work out and we will be steered to another path. Our prayers tell us this is so:

Thy will be done.

Once we are mature enough to understand that we may want the best for ourselves and others but we don't always know what best is, *Thy will be done* takes on a whole new meaning.

Practice: In Harmony with the Greater Good

Sit quietly and communicate with the spirit of things to begin a sense of what you want and the knowledge of who you really are. In time, if you practice prayer and quiet reflection, thy will and my will will increasingly align. You may continue your same projects or dreams but with the feeling that you are acting in harmony with the greater good. You will know through prayer when this is happening because you will feel no division between yourself and your spirit. The two of you are holding hands moving through time. You might start by chanting:

Spirit of all. Spirit of all.

Sometimes unanswered prayers are the best outcome. Think of a friend in a destructive relationship who wishes and prays for the spouse's return. When we hear someone praying for what they want and not what their life needs, we can help them by praying for the best outcome for them and hope that in time they may come to see that love must serve life and allow them to live that life happily in balance.

We all deserve happiness and harmony. So be it.

Direct or indirect prayer, both are needed to make your life more connected to your spirit and to better connect to those you love.

CHAPTER 8

✤

Prayers for Clarifying Our Beliefs and Goals

As long as there is hunger and poverty, there is work to do. The Spiritual way is to change the systems so that all human beings can live with dignity and live in peace and harmony. We can bring that about if we work to make it happen. You've got to work for the good. I'm working for the creator. I refuse to take part of anything that would destroy what the creator has made.

TADODALO CHIEF LEON SHENDOL, QUOTED IN STEVE WALL'S
TO BECOME A HUMAN BEING

One of the most powerful ways of clarifying our own beliefs is through prayer. We ask:

Let my path be known to me.
Let me see the way.
Under my pen, my feelings known.
Let feelings lead the way to truth.
I ask that I trust how I feel.
I ask to know the best for all.
I listen. I question. I believe. I listen. I question. I believe.

Practice: Clarify Your Beliefs

Write down some simple prayer you might say to help clarify your beliefs. Chant if you want to.

Prayer is also a wonderful vehicle for expressing those beliefs. As we pray we can ask, Does this prayer reflect my beliefs? Does this prayer open new ways of thinking for me into which I want to step? Do I believe in the message? Does it resonate to a part of me that I don't know about yet and can I choose it in faith?

Those who practice Wicca, the ancient earth-based religion that embraces magic and mystery, often practice rituals to help ground them in spirit. You might want to try a modified Wiccan ritual yourself.

Practice: Becoming Grounded in Spirit

Gather a group of friends in a circle, preferably outdoors. Declare sacred ground, call in the four directions of air, fire, water, and earth to bring in energy, and try saying the following:

In this circle, we place ourselves as boughs blowing in the wind and plants that seed the earth. We call the fire of the sun to fuel our lives and waters to sweep over our wrongdoings. We ask stone to hold good firm in our hearts, and, in the hard land of earth, find a cold surface of slate to cool the heat of May. Fed from plains of crown corn growing, we pray: Oh God, oh Goddess, blessed be.

At this point you might wash your hands in a communal bowl and take a stone from the bottom of the bowl to use as a reminder of spirit everywhere.

Practice: Starting a Self-Discovery Journal

If you are unsure of what you believe, you might want to start a journal of self-discovery. In the journal write just as fast as you can the ideas and feelings you are tossing around in your consciousness. I call it streaming. This technique was detailed in my book *Stirring the Waters: Writing to Find Your Spirit:* Just start writing across the page. Keep going. Write your name if you don't know what else to write. Continue without much thinking. Don't stop. Make doodles to fill in the lines if you have nothing to say. Pay no attention to the inner critic. This is your time to wonder. This is a time to be curious and explore. After several minutes of being 'present' with your writing you'll find you're in a shift. You've really let go and are just writing. Keep going. After you've written for fifteen minutes or more, go back and underline insights and anything you'd like to continue at another time.

Allow yourself to continue until it feels right to stop. Go back and reread what you have written and see what the core of the writing holds. Are there images that you would like to take with you into prayer? Is there a question? An asking for something unseen? Here are some questions you might want to ask yourself. Some of these will become clear immediately or in time, others will remain unanswered until a life experience helps you find the answer. Some questions may go with you to the death journey and be raised again in spirit form.

Practice: Questions to Help You Clarify Your Beliefs

- Do you believe in a spiritual energy outside of yourself? What would you call it? Where is this energy?
- What is the difference between a God and your spiritual belief if you have one? How does that work for you?
- What is your best self and how does that fit in with your spirituality?
- What is your spiritual purpose? The purpose of your life?
- What are the activities that quiet you or nurture prayer in your life?
- What can your prayer life give you? What can you give your prayer life?
- Do your beliefs lead you to live a life of joy, beauty, love, and openness?

Once you start praying actively, you will find that many of these questions are answered. You have taken yourself into the arena of spirituality and nothing cared for and nurtured stays the same. By our attention, we create change and clarity.

Clarifying Your Goals

Prayer can also be an important ally in helping you clarify your goals, and if you want to improve the quality of your life, setting goals is one good way to do that. Studies have shown that people who have written goals are much more likely to achieve what they want both personally and in business. It's also refreshing to the spirit when you are clear about who *you* are and what *you* want, and not just what the market or your family or your role dictates you *should* want and need. I use the following format to help myself and clients clarify our goals.

Practice: Clarifying Your Values
We carry our values close to our heart and out of our values, we choose our goals.

Clarifying Values
I am _____. (values)
I choose _____. (goal)
I create _____. (activities)
I do _____. (schedule)

Here is an example of what one client did with this exercise to help her at work: "I am outgoing and joyful. I am spiritual and kind. I chose to work in public relations for an environmental concern. I create (write) press releases for Save Our Forests for all the major media on my list. I do this work by Friday noon, the 14th of September."

She said she likes to look at her list because it reminds her, on tough days, why she's in public relations: meeting people and going to various meetings and activities for the environment, being out and about in her community, working with issues about which she is passionate. At the end of the day, she feels her work, though a drop in the bucket, is one more drop of good energy for the planet.

Another client worked with this exercise this way: I am a spiritual person. I choose to pray each morning and night and go to a prayer group with the Quakers on Sunday mornings.

I create a quiet space for myself alone and with other people with my values. I do my prayers every morning and evening for twenty minutes and go to the Quaker meeting every Sunday at 10 a.m. I live my life in quiet harmony.

Practice: Clarifying Your Goals

You might want to begin a spiritual journal and try the following exercise:

Clarifying Your Goals

1 List what you don't want.

2 List what you should want. Who says?

3 What hasn't lived yet in your life?

4 What have you always wanted to do?

5 What would you do if you could do anything you wanted for a year after travel and resting?

6 Name important elements you want in these areas of your life: spiritual, friendships, family, significant other, creativity, financial, health, planet, others. (For purposes of this exercise, we split your life into important elements. In time, all elements of your life will be a reflection of spirituality in action.)

7 Set a timeline that makes room for the most significant elements in each area and see if you can come up with a goal, activity, and schedule for these. Keep this list in your schedule book and refer to it daily to make sure you are on track. Make sure one activity in each area is prayer – direct or indirect.

Pay attention to your day and night dreams for clues about what is important to you. Notice clues in your envy. (Release the envy and keep the desire.) Notice clues in dissatisfactions and ask, "What do I want?" Listen to your intuition and what the authentic essence of you wants and enjoys. Ask your spirit to guide you and keep checking on the balance in your life goals. Allow yourself in prayer to feel gratitude for what you have today and for your progress. Share your abundance today with others acknowledging the help of the spirit.

If you have an aversion to setting goals, allow yourself to feel your fear, doubt, helplessness, anger, and sadness for the times in the past that you have set goals that did not come to pass. You may have to allow yourself to feel whatever comes up from having set goals in a dysfunctional way, or from having had unrealistic

> expectations or goals that did not reflect who you are. Your prayer life will help you forgive yourself for your conflicted feelings.
>
> *Always I am beginning anew again.*

I once set goals to be a photographer and, after schooling, setting up my own laboratory, and showing thirty-seven prints in a one-woman show, I had to face the fact that I hated to be alone in the dark all day. I hadn't been paying attention to my spirit. I value artistic expression but I forgot about my need for people and connection.

Although I love images and the capturing of real life in photography, writing is a better way for me to feel my spirit in the day-to-day process of doing it. Writing isn't as lonely for me as photography because I write in a room with a lovely view of trees and have the ability to write with others around. Writing brings me a connection in a way the chemical processes in the dark room couldn't. At the time, I didn't see this as a spiritual issue – I wasn't aware of my spirituality at all then and didn't have a prayer life – but I could feel I needed creative expression.

Looking back, I see that creativity was a way to my spirit and my sense of a spirit of good in the world.

As I create, I am in spirit.

Sometimes we pray in search of communion. Other times we want to listen or to be heard. Whether we pray to express wonder, longing, or transformation, by praying we make our needs more visible and that is a good thing. Since prayer is the natural language of love and the heart, just to pray stretches those muscles and that may be the most important goal of all.

Prayers for When We Feel Lost

⚜

Many of us also turn to prayer when nothing feels right and we have lost our spirits. "I felt so unhappy," a friend once told me, "when I found myself with eight weeks of work ahead and not one day to myself. It wasn't anyone's fault really. It was my father's birthday, I had several scheduled talks and a conference, my boyfriend had scheduled back shoulder surgery, and I had more work at the office because of a recent merger.

"By the sixth week I felt frayed at the edges. I could feel myself looking for someone to blame. I wasn't sleeping well and felt like I couldn't take a deep breath. 'Anxious,' my friends said. 'As if I didn't know that,' I thought! Finally, one night I stumbled out to the bathroom to put Chapstick™ on my lips and I ended up putting white under-eye cream on my mouth. Tim said I looked like a clown and thought I was playing. I felt hurt and looked in the mirror. Having no sense of humor at that moment, I cried. I dreamt I was screaming in my sleep that night. The next morning I knew I was over the top even though the busy times were about over. I finally remembered to start praying again."

She came into my office and after she told me her story I said that I wanted us to sit together and pray silently and see what images or feelings came. She saw herself splashing herself with fresh water and said, "Thank God."

Then she relaxed and said, "Space," then, "desert flower." Then she sighed, "Bloom." Together we imagined her on a desert with life all around but the kind of life only a close eye would notice. It was enough for now. She found her prayer:

Blooming now.

Given her time and resources, she probably would have done little different during those eight weeks except take some time for herself to burn a candle and pray. Perhaps she could have reminded herself that she was spirit and spirit was all around and this was a time to *be in* and not *get over*. Perhaps she could have felt the spirit listening and providing solace.

As for screaming, she would have asked for more emotional help with the care of her boyfriend. Whether he was a great patient or not, she was the one who needed an outlet.

Practice: Knowing Yourself Better

Try saying a prayer to know yourself better. In your notebook you might want to have various headings for prayers such as "Returning to Myself" and prayers you use such as:

I am cocooned with my spirit.
I know who I am.

I know when I am hungry or angry or lonely or tired, I forget I have much of a spiritual life and feel alone and crabby. More and more, I can remember to name what I am feeling and why, and let myself be joined in spirit prayer:

Here I am, a wreck. Be with me.

And then I take care of myself. It's better to name what's going on than to stay confused and lose perspective. It's better to pray and know all situations pass and know I am in the flux of things.

Here I am taking care.

There are times when we feel lost and feel separated from ourselves and our spirit. We know this is happening because we don't know how we feel. It helps to remember that we don't have to have everything figured out. We can just sit in the knowledge that we don't know how we feel. However, we may know that we wish we could touch the light in the trees and ride it and say a prayer about that. That is a start.

A few lines from a poem I wrote might help you find contentment knowing you are part of a group growing in numbers whether you pray alone or not.

God circles this place on the map, and says,
You are right here and it is important.
All over the world people
gather to polish the rock
raised from the warm Atlantic, lifted from the red fishes

of the Pacific, picked up at the
doorway of work. Groups attend to the green circle
not questioning what is given but trees and rivers
and a body of words on the tongue.

Recently, I went with a group called Wilderness Women to a youth hostel at Pigeon Point, about fifty minutes south of San Francisco. The hostel is perched on a cliff and was constructed in 1872 after several shipwrecks happened there, including the wreck of the Carrier Pigeon where the ship was destroyed but the crew was saved. I learned that each lighthouse has its own light pattern that captains can find in their Light List book to help determine their location. I sat in the hot tub at the top of the thirty-five-foot cliff that night and thought about those patterns. I wondered if we each give out our distinctive light to the spirit that holds us all.

Thank you for noticing my light.

When we feel lost, we can give some simple thanks.

Thank you for your light.
Thank you for listening.

Practice: Lost and Found
Write a story of a person lost and found. Is there a lesson in this for you to note?

Sometimes prayer helps us clarify and strengthen our boundaries which helps us feel less vulnerable and lost. It can help us stay relaxed in the midst of other people's aggression or anxiety. Think of the guy who cuts you off on the freeway. Having a way of centering yourself through prayer can help you not get hooked into his aggression. You can then choose to stay calm. Prayer, practiced regularly, allows us to live from our center and not be so reactive to others. This gives us the opportunity to watch how our minds move their attention to others; then we can *choose* whether to respond.

It's so easy to operate from an "other-oriented" pattern, but when we do we often give too much of ourselves away and do not allow ourselves to know ourselves well. We'd probably prefer to be free from much that is not our business anyway. We can take our issues to prayer.

Help me care and yet be separate.

A student of mine, Kala, told me that sometimes she thinks she gets too hooked into other people's feelings. She has a friend, for example, who used to talk a lot about her problems at work. *Everything* reminded her friend of the stressful politics at her workplace and Kala found herself listening more than she wanted to. She thought about it and took it to prayer. Inner guidance told her that the friendship was worth the risk of honesty so she gently told her friend that sometimes it was hard to listen to all her work problems.

It was awkward, of course, but far preferable to disappearing from her friend's life. It even stayed awkward for awhile, but her friend became more careful about the time and attention for which she asked, and gradually they worked it out so that they'd both vent for the first few minutes they were together and then go and have a good time.

Kala didn't have to avoid her friend; she didn't have to be mad. Through prayer she claimed her boundaries and asked for something she needed.

Kala's friend eventually said that she likes not worrying about her because she'll speak up if anything is wrong and so will she. She also said that she was glad she felt strong enough inside to take the criticism and that there would have been times in her life that she couldn't have heard that she was taking up too much time with her worries without feeling wronged.

Give me friends I can trust.

Practice: Centering

If you have access to a tape recorder or CD burner, record the following, then play it back, eyes closed. Just let the words wash over you:

There is a seed in you that is your center. It is your spiritual center and is the place where your love sprouts and grows. It lies in the heart, in the deepest place of your being where love is never ending. It is the place where love can find protection, love can find its root, love can find its wings to grow. This is your center. This is the place in you that holds heart with harmony. This is the place in which you matter. From your heart, you are centered.

You are in a green growing place of love. Love starts with you and shines its face on you. Love loves you. Love spreads to your neighbors, to the world. You are centered. You are love. You are centered in the wonder of love.

Try these practices and just see which ones you respond to. I think you'll find that it takes almost no time at all to get to the place of love. What takes time is just getting to the thought and the belief that it's important enough to do.

❧

CHAPTER 9

Prayers for Emotional Healing

Just me,

sitting in the boil of anger looking for spirit.

Let spirit find me. Here!

One of the most powerful uses of prayer is as a healer of difficult emotions. Through prayer we can find our way to stability as we release our anger, ask for forgiveness, dry our tears, and find the joy that belongs to us. It is hard work to learn to be aware of our feelings and the behaviors that accompany them. But, sooner or later, we must understand which feelings and behaviors are not serving us. We cannot be in touch with our spirit if we don't know our feelings because the spirit soars on authenticity.

If we are angry, we can ask to be healed of anger and resentment. If we are disappointed we can ask for grace. We can look back at family of origin issues and see what first made us angry and connect with how that gets triggered in life today. We can then agree on behaviors that would better serve us and practice, practice, practice.

Prayer practice,
that's what this is.
I bring a longing to prayer.

We use prayer to bow to mystery of what we don't understand about others and ourselves and we raise our eyes to the horizon to watch the day in the opening pink of its flower. It is this new vision of life and what we may be that is one of the great gifts of prayer.

After eighteen years of private practice as a therapist I know that the first step to healing anger is to become aware of our anger issues. Just to know what we think, feel, and do that hurts us and others helps us heal. For instance, a client, Marie, felt that two important people in her life had distanced from her just when she needed them most. Gradually, she came to see that she had trouble with depression and when depressed, she had unreasonable expectations of her friends. At her most negative, she wanted complete agreement.

When Marie could accept that she held some responsibility for friends retreating she had the chance to create something new. In this case, it was to tell her friends that she was depressed and it was hard for her not to believe that everything was awful. She could ask for their support to remind her that it was depression talking and not the vision of the world she supported. She could use her prayer practice to release the anger that depression holds just by sitting with herself in love and the world of spirit:

Even this feeling in me I can love.

Another example comes to mind. A young man in his twenties came to see me. He was a binge drinker and had broken his foot for the fourth time in ten years. He didn't think he was an alcoholic but his wife insisted he get some help.

It became apparent that he would go on these drunken weekends to release a lot of pent-up anger. His anger would escalate to a such a level of rage that he would pound his foot into the wall. Many times he didn't break anything but just suffered some bruises or twists to his ankle or foot. Four times he actually broke bones and now he had done permanent damage and needed surgery.

He was finally ready to see that he was using his drinking as a way of self-medicating. He needed to stop drinking immediately and learn to vent as situations happened rather than waiting for an anger eruption resembling a volcano.

I talked to him about letting his anger out, like a leaking faucet, but in a kind way, and then used hypnotherapy, a process that by-passes the conscious mind and goes into the subconscious and dreaming, to help him relax and go into a focused state. I repeated positive suggestions and asked him to stay focused and relaxed as he listened to what I was saying and to let himself feel what I said.

I am a good person and have all my feelings including anger.
It's safe to be mad.
I leak anger out as it comes up.
I turn my attention to myself sometimes.
I express my feelings with love.
I express anger. Day to day. Little ways.
People love me even though I tell my truth.

In every way every day I am getting more authentic.
I don't hurt myself or others with my anger.
I learn to be compassionate with my anger.

I then gave him a list of what I had said and asked him to add to it for the next session. Because he had been brought up in a church he still attended, I asked him to start a practice of repeating the following prayer.

I am a good person
even if I have anger.
I can express my anger in the every day
in a kind way.

With prayer we are asking the deepest part of ourselves, our spiritual being, to step in and help. Prayer is saying, *I accept that I need help.* I don't know how to do this myself. Through prayer we ask to be led to a better way.

Spirit, I accept your guidance.

You can trust yourself and where you are on your journey. You can remember your childhood and decide to return to heart-felt prayers such as:

Keep me safe.

Through prayer we can learn to release anger in compassionate ways that communicate our feelings but do not punish or teach a lesson. I call this compassionate anger.

I am responsible to feel and express. I do so without injuring others.

The Navajos had a solution to violent dreams or evil thoughts which was to perform a ritual with sand paintings and prayer chants and paraphernalia which would absorb the evil images and thoughts. It was ignorance, they believed, that caused evil, so they told the story of creation during the ritual to give the person knowledge of their connection to the whole to help release anger and feel connected to their origin. A chant might go like this:

Tell stories and I come.
Tell stories and I come.
I sit under the sun and the sun shines bright.
I pull on the cloud and the cloud gives rain.
With plenty of food from the earth, I sing.
I sing again with a belly full of corn.
I am the sun and the cloud and the rain.
I am the food and the earth.
I am the corn.

It is interesting to me to know that each of the world's major religions has a form of the Golden Rule of the Christian Bible which says that we should not do to others what we would not do to ourselves. Baha'i: Do not lay on any soul a load which you would not wish to be laid upon yours. Buddhism: Do not hurt others in a way that you yourself would find hurtful. Hinduism: Never do to others what would pain thyself. Native American: The foundation for all life is respect. Islam: Wish for your brother what you wish for yourself. Judaism: Treat all creatures as we wish to be treated, in joy and grief, happiness and suffering.

All of these would actually be good prayers for you to practice and would help you heal the feelings of vengeance or retaliation that can arise from the heat of anger.

We must recognize ourselves as humans who make mistakes and find it hard to say we're sorry and recognize the toll that takes on our mind, body, and spirit.

My client, Bill, tells me he doesn't even know he is holding his breath when angry but he is and then he feels anxious. Here are some steps you can take to release your anger:

• Admit to it.
• Tell someone and write about it.
• Remember the good this person has done for you.
• Remember the good in the world and think of loving people.
• Pray to forgive and give the other person a gift/message, saying:

I forgive myself. I forgive you. I understand shortcomings. I understand misunderstandings. I understand myself in human nature.

(If this is difficult at first, focus on the gift or message. I often use flowers and find that the flowers match the energy of the person – roses for deep hurt, daisies for carelessness, lily for seriousness, jasmine for love.)

Through a prayer practice we come to realize that there is a life energy within us that holds every cloud, every misdeed, every gentle wind of hope. We are where the world begins and ends, and we can make a difference. If we see ourselves as but a seed of healing, we create energy that is good for the world. It is up to us to open our hearts to pray to be the best self we can be.

You are the best part of me.

Flames of Forgiveness

We can also use our prayer practice to forgive – both ourselves and others.

It can be very hard to forgive someone who has seen us at our worst. We hold this against them out of shame or embarrassment. A client, Bet, told me how she acted petty and jealous with a new friend and broke off the friendship. Looking back she recognized that she wasn't getting much from the friendship and wanted to break it off, but she didn't like the way she became careless in her emotional responses and created a more dramatic break. When she saw her ex-friend she felt embarrassed yet didn't want to get close.

Bet decided to forgive herself in her prayer practice and prayed to release her disappointment that the friendship didn't work and her poor behavior that ended the relationship. She prayed to accept that she was human. In the end, Bet called the other woman to say she was sorry for becoming mad about scheduling and acting difficult. They didn't become friends again but Bet felt better about herself and perhaps she helped the other woman let go of any feelings of negativity too.

> *As I am,*
> *not perfect.*
> *As I try to be,*
> *better.*

Not being able to forgive gets in the way of getting on with our lives. You can't start a new relationship and really be there, if you are furious at your ex – and don't trust others not to betray you. So, here's an exercise that will enter your prayers:

Practice: An Exercise in Self-Forgiveness

Imagine making a mistake; now visualize redoing the interaction as you wished you had – with more compassion. Say a prayer to yourself from this exercise: I apologize to myself. Now I apologize to _____, knowing I am truly sorry. (This helps even if the other doesn't take your apology with grace.)

Families can be particularly hard to forgive because we want so much from them and childhood feelings of hurt and anger are well established. If, for example, you want to be an artist but you know that your family pattern is to revere intellect, chances are you will bump up against their values. By knowing and even respecting this, you are in a better position to pursue a different path without taking their disagreement personally.

You can let them know how it feels to you without raging or making them wrong, sticking to your feelings instead of telling them what they are doing to hurt you, "I feel hurt that my art doesn't seem important to you. It's what I do best and it's what I want to spend my life exploring. Even if there's not much money in art, I bring beauty into the world and I'd like some emotional support for that."

A prayer to deal with the family's lack of support might be:

> *Let each be seen for their good contribution.*
> *May I be seen and valued.*
> *May I see and value my work.*
> *Spirit, may I connect with you.*

I met a woman at a brunch yesterday and we started talking about family reunions. She told me that reunions are finally fun for her. When she was younger, she'd go and notice the differences and how she wasn't respected or supported for her choices. The family liked her in spite of her wanderlust and didn't see that she was living her life in search of meaning. She never really wanted a career but was always self-supporting as she explored the world. Now, she's able to go to family reunions and see similarities to her family and finds herself saying to herself: "These are people with my blood. I started here. My father is the oldest here and won't live much longer. Listen and connect to what he has to say."

Her outsider status is less important to her now that she has matured and has others to witness her life in positive ways. Her Buddhist practice of meditation and personal prayer has helped a great deal too because she feels connected to generations of people searching for their Buddha nature.

We all are the same and different.
I choose to be here
with my family.

"Forgiveness is the economy of the heart ... Forgiveness saves the expense of anger, the cost of hatred, the waste of spirits," writes Hannah More in 1811, in *Practical Piety*. Lack of forgiveness keeps irritability and anger in our bodies. It makes us bitter people; we can feel justified in holding on but it doesn't help our spirit. I often think that I try to forgive for the selfish reason that it makes me feel better. When I feel better, I am closer to my spiritual nature and no longer long for connection: I am connected:

Always with spirit or about to be.

If prayer is nothing more than a yearning of the heart, then yearn in prayer for forgiveness. You may have to do this again and again for the same issue, until the energy is released. That's fine. We learn in finite measures, a step at a time how to find compassion for others and ourselves and then our hearts are filled with love – for a minute, a day, a season until we return and ask the spirit to once again make us whole with ourselves.

When I can no longer stand
the flesh of my anger reddened and seething
holding on to grievances and every wrongdoing,
and I am most in hatred,
I ask rescue.

This is my prayer:
a journey where life flows through me,
felt and accepted, moving
like the turning seasons, the storm that harms or nourishes
but passes.

This is my prayer:
grace with forgiveness,
an arrow shot through the storm to sun and light.

Prayers for Release

I listened to a friend last night as she talked of failed efforts to form a group with whom to sing. This had extra meaning because she regretted not having the self-esteem to take the risk and develop a singing career when she was young; the seeds of hurt in her were just too deep and well-watered by the consistency of abuse from her childhood to make her try anything risky then.

Today she knows to ask for loving support for her feelings and finds disappointment thinning with the sharing. She knows the future doesn't always make up for the past: however, she realizes she'll be delivered to a new place of healing by her efforts to release her regret and that would have blessings of its own. Her life is a prayer of being in balance, doing what's best and what she can, and praying:

Let me accept my journey.

Betrayal is a part of life; people let us down. People are also wonderful to us and are loyal. To name the events and feel the feelings all the way through, to have that process witnessed by someone else, to take it to prayer is one way to eliminate the pain although it may take time.

Betrayal can take all our prayers, for when we have trusted someone who has been unfaithful, it not only affects the relationship but trust in our own judgment often making us doubt ourselves.

Nadine Gordimer powerfully writes of betrayal in her book, *The Lying Days,* "I saw this thing turn, like a flower, once picked turning petals into bright knives in your hand. And it was so much desired, so lovely that your fingers will not loosen, and you have only disbelief that this, of all you have ever known, should have the possibility of pain."

Betrayal is difficult to release because it intersects hurt and anger. You may need to cry and beat pillows and scream at the ocean or in your car, take responsibility for your part, and then pray:

Release me from hurt. Release me from feelings of revenge.
Release anger from my body. Let me give this to you, spirit,
so I can be free.

Let my prayers take me deep into myself so that I might find
I possess exactly what I desire.

Loss through death is sometimes easier to deal with because the loved one did not leave you purposely. Life and death happen. When a loved one dies it is often the grief connected with pleasant memories of every day things that is unnoticed by others but hard for us. To walk into a room and see your husband's favorite reading place or sister's music box can cause a flood of grief:

Help me live through this.

I once felt a grief that felt like panic. I felt mute and wanted time to go backwards, take me back to the place of hope and dreaming.

I am asked to accept the unacceptable and I don't know how. Help me.

Gradually I worked through the grief and learned that there is a danger of trying to suppress and escape our past instead of integrating its opposing elements. For even when the past and its pain appears miles behind, it will not let you go and suddenly when you don't feel it is close at all it is right there next to you, all in a moment.

Gentleness, kindness, and tears of release, time and even therapy really help. Anger intermingled with the tears acts as a release and a balm. Prayer. Open and honest expression. Life is not fair and we must understand that again and again. Life is not measured that way!

As I live, I find a way.

When you feel empty and depleted with no direction and nowhere to go, you can turn and pray in the emptiness, in the void of the dark silent pond at night until the day brings the chirping life around the pond and gurgling sounds of life. After awhile prayer may help release you from pain's clutches and you will find you are not held so tightly a captive.

There will be times when you are caught in the tide pull of feeling that seems to do no one any good. That is not true. It's human to feel deep loss. It shows that you have desire, that you are vulnerable. It shows that the footprints of past loss and hurt, traces left on the imprint of your heart that say, "Nothing works out" can turn – can slowly, then with more vigor, like a top twirling – change to prayers for guidance.

I do not have to understand. Guide me, spirit. Hold me,
rock me.

At a reading last winter, poet Mark Doty talked about fertilizing grief with a bone and a fish. He meant to encourage grief if that's what you need to feel. He talked about losing his lover and the state of fresh grief where poetry can be too contained for such oceanic feelings. He turns to prose. I think of prayer as something able to hold the uncontainable, and how writing can help in the grief process as a visual sign making grief real. Then, prayers can fly those prayers to the spirit alive.

All things in life,
death, return, my life.

The year my best friend died I asked why of everything; I wanted the world to be thrown to my feet in answers. Those early days I felt like I couldn't manage a journey so delicately webbed. I wrote much poetry to help me vent feelings and to try to make something of someone gone. The poetry also helped me know what I was feeling because it would come out under my hands as if my fingers were alive.

> *My prayers say her breath belonged to her,*
> *that each of us has the right not to suffer.*
> *Her life, she'd want you to remember,*
> *was filled with years of song and taffy.*

With the help of poetry and prayer I realized sometimes troubles are beyond solution and no one deserves such suffering. I could only ask for grace to walk with me and try to bring it home to her through my prayers. And I knew her spirit, no matter how burdened, always had grace for me.

> *Blessed be, _____ in the trees and hillsides. Let me know*
> *you are with me as I am with you.*

It seemed impossible that she would become so troubled (later I learned it was advanced Addison's Disease) and I felt unsafe. It felt like the near-by bay could hurl its water up the legs of my house, bury velvet chair, and fill broom closets, I realized the life I knew to be my story was gone. I felt homeless! I walked to the shore and sat on the rocks to hear holy prayer from my body. I felt the rocks silent, cold, and unwelcoming. I felt alone with grief.

This death felt harder in some ways than losing the babies because I knew the death of the babies were beyond my control. During the year of my friend's death, not understanding it was an adrenaline gland disorder, I felt I wasn't helping enough. I had time to "fix" it but I couldn't. Maybe, I thought, I wasn't being a good enough friend or doing it right.

I needed some kind of connection and turned to a prayer group for people who had lost loved ones in difficult circumstances. I heard tales of nests full of stones, lost mates and children, the eggs of their hearts broken. It was pain that made me belong; we all wanted resurrection from the pain.

I learned if you have suffered a deep loss, you can let yourself imagine you can touch the light in the trees and ride it. You can realize your loved one's spirit could be in the trees. With prayer, you may come to believe that you don't have to understand. Pray for happiness of life, an acceptance of this death, and forgiving yourself. Believe your loved one will become a nonphysical spirit always alive in the world, and pray.

Pray for your loved one to be in a gentle wood and feel her spirit near. Let the time come when your loved one seems settled among the blowing grasses and even the tree outside your office. Feel her spirit. Let her be part of your spirit life and prayer life. Let a yearning begin to build new ground, life expanding itself. I wrote in part of a poem, "like a fist opening and closing, like a wind that lifts us up and swings us around and sets us back down again, so the spirit moves."

Native American Indians have a kind of prayer that does nothing but release the lament of sorrow. The purpose of the prayer is to put the words into the world for the great spirit to hear and relieve you of your suffering. It is also an opportunity to vent your feelings and move on. The prayer is done in a repetitive way through the night.

Lonely. I am lonely, I wail. I wait.

By living a symbolic life, by being willing to believe in spirits in the trees, that happiness will come to your life again as humming-birds, you'll enrich your life, your prayers, and your spirituality.

As I pray, I become.

Prayer says we believe in something we cannot see but that does not make it less real. If you need to, when doubt comes, dig a hole in the ground and say, "There, a scar I can see." When you believe in yourself again, you feel that scar and don't care as much if others see it or believe in your journey. It's real and you can take it to prayer.

With our personal prayers from the heart, we can decide how we want to show love to our departed ones. Will you ask your family to join you on your departed loved one's birthday or the day of their death? Will you set up a ritual of lighting a candle and praying alone or together or ask someone to read something in remembrance? Will you pray to string the pearls back to your ancient ancestors? It's up to you if and how you want to do it. All that is important is that you decide what to do to deepen love and connection.

You are remembered with love and respect. You are part of the common thread that binds us together. You are part of the tribe. We, together.

The custom of praying for the dead is a part of many traditions. The Celts had a custom of soul-caring, where the children go house to house asking for sweet cakes in return for prayers for the souls of the village's departed ones. This was done up to the nineteenth century and shows respect and connects the innocence of childhood with ancestors and time eternal.

Young and old, life continuing.

In a recent trip to New Orleans I went on a cemetery tour. Because the land is below sea level much of the year, families buy plots and bury their dead on top of each other. It is a law in New Orleans that the bones of the dead cannot be removed for a year and a day to insure that the body has turned to dust. At that point, the oldest can be moved to the front section of the grave to co-mingle with other family members. On the grave sites are written traditional prayers:

Blessed are the dead, souls in peace.

In other parts of New Orleans you find the practice of the Voodoo religion where people believe in one supreme God but many spirits or Loas to whom they pray. Ancestors are revered and consulted for guidance and protection. The prayers are often in requests such as for food and money:

Feed our mouths just as you feed our spirits, this oh Loas, we beg.

I find myself being interested in all prayer and realize that prayer leads me many places where I otherwise would not be. I explore the Voodoo Museum and hear African drums pounding as practitioners search for ancient roots and wisdom:

Spirit, the many drums you hear are our wishes to find you.

To pray with "zero church" is to voice an interconnection of life and all its triggers of past hurt and longings. It threads back in history to all people who turned to the spirit. In our new way of prayer we connect with the lover, the spouse, the past, the future, the friends, the faithful, and the betrayers of trust, and those who open their hands and heart to us.

When we feel empty and depleted with no direction and nowhere to go, we turn and pray in the emptiness.

I held on to all my losses like stones in my pockets until, one day at the bank of the river, I saw moss and mud clinging to stone and realized stones belonged to the world and not me.

Emptying my pockets at the river's edge, my heart lightened. I felt a freedom. With the damp body of nature turned toward me, I felt a breeze of promise returning.

In prayer, we can ask to accept life on life's terms. There are many things in our life we will not get to do. We may never learn to horseback ride and gallop down the beach, the wind wild in our hair. We may never get to Paris or try on fancy hats. And yet, we are given plenty over which to rejoice: our breath and a life filled with family and friendship, laughter plentifully spilling from the little mishaps of the day.

I long for promise returning.
Let me feel the breeze.

There are dreams that will be answered and dreams that will go unanswered. Sometimes we will get our way, other times we will be asked to stay awhile in the dark forest of pain. We may learn difficult lessons from the denial of a great love or desire. We may try to push the boulder up the hill only to have it roll down again the minute we look the other way.

We will never know if unanswered prayers were left undone because they were not best for us or the world. Not for sure. We never know the whole picture; the vision for the world is beyond us. We can only rarely feel how we affect the way the world turns. There is no one answer or one sure thing.

You have a choice in some of your paths – some chosen, some destiny – and prayer is a path that can help you become one with your spirit. Through prayer you have a chance to live as you are living only more so. The world can look like itself outside while we hold a different landscape inside; a landscape of hills and valleys held in God's arms. We can walk the cement sidewalks yet be carried.

The spirit holds me as I walk the earth.

Finding Joy Through Prayer

❦

There is a way in which prayer brings us directly to our joy. Distress comes when we feel unsettled or when we don't quite know how we feel but connecting to spirit allows us to drop right down to our center of joy. I think of the times when I feel disconnected from my partner and yet don't know what is wrong, only to realize days later that I was fretting over clients and classes and I wasn't connected to my spirit. When I am off center, I worry about image and the content and how I am doing. When I find myself doing this, I use this awareness to shift my attention to love and contribution, my spirit's call.

As we pray we begin to recover the knowledge that to be alive is to be intoxicated with joy. There is nothing to be saved from, no struggle against the world, no God to please or to be feared. As activist and spiritual teacher Starhawk writes in *The Spiral Dance*, "The other, the turning spiral that whirls us in and out of existence, whose winking eye is the pulse of being – birth, death, rebirth – whose laughter bubbles and courses through all things and who is found only in love: love of trees, of stones, of sky and clouds, or scented blossoms and thundering waves; of all that runs and flies and swims and crawls on her face; through love of ourselves."

The circle is open, but unbroken. May the peace of the Goddess go on in our hearts; merry meet, and merry part. And merry meet again. Blessed be.

It's not excitement prayer brings but joy. Joy, centered in our bodies so we may live and love and work and do the everyday. Prayer becomes the communication of joy from in our bodies to the world and out to spirit. It is our vehicle for the joy of connection.

There are several wonderful quotations about joy that I keep in my address book so I can remember to reach for joy that is given me in the everyday. Mother Theresa said, "Joy is a net of love by which you can catch souls," and in her *Times to Remember*, written a year after JFK died, Rose Kennedy wrote, "Birds sing after a storm; why shouldn't people feel as free to delight in whatever sunlight remains to them?" I also carry these words from Helen Keller, "Joy is the holy fire that keeps our purpose warm and our intelligence aglow."

All of these quotations suggest that joy springs from a depth within. We can connect to this energy pool of life through prayer.

Prayer, my longing for fresh waters.

An old Louisiana Creole proverb says it, too: "Tell me who you love and I'll tell you who you are."

Try it and see who you are.

CHAPTER 10

꙰

Prayers for Physical Healing

How can I honor my body when I am sick and hurting?
Ask the spirit to keep me company and pray for ease.

In the September 2002 issue of *Spirituality and Health* magazine, Bernie Siegel wrote that a 1990 study at Ohio State:
"found psychological stress can switch off our genes so that our
white blood cells have no receptors to be able to recognize
foreign bacteria and viruses, let alone fight them … Even bacteria are able to make intelligent genetic changes and resist
antibiotics. They are here to do God's work, too, and they have
fewer problems to think about."

Siegel's work suggests that when our consciousness is peaceful, and we lead a life with compassion and love, our body
receives a powerful message: *live*. Prayer helps us find this
peace and transcend our physical limitations. It allows us to
reach beyond human consciousness. This calling is a deepening
of spirit connection that allows us to reach the mysterious
energies that usually lie just beyond our reach.

Using our vehicle of prayer to communicate to our spirit is a
way of healing ourselves in whatever way we can – sometimes the

body and other times the mind-body-spirit connection, so that we may face our future with an attitude of acceptance and grace. Siegel urges us to get support from the people in our lives and to use that support to help heal others and ourselves. Louise Erdrich in her book *Tracks* writes, "I got well by talking. Death could not get a word in edgewise, grew discouraged, and traveled on."

Although some things in life are beyond measure, there have been a number of studies documenting the positive effects of prayer on physical healing. This is not to say that illness is a spiritual problem or a mind-produced problem. That would be blaming the ill one who needs only compassion and love. What it does tell us is that there is mystery in prayer and that mystery might help us heal.

In his book *Courage to Pray*, Anthony Bloom states, "Interceding prayer means to place ourselves at the heart of a troubled situation." This is also what I feel about working on the emotional component of illness these eighteen years as a hypnotherapist: I work to find the heart of the troubled situation and in that place add positive suggestions and hope.

For instance, a client, Naomi, with rheumatoid arthritis came to me in great pain. After listening to her story, I had the sense that she was disappointed and angry with life. I knew she was afraid, too, but she used the words *brittle* and *cracking* and said, "I'm all used up, dry and tired of life." Her story and words didn't always make a lot of sense to me but I had the strong intuitive feeling if she could find hope again, she would have, at the least, less pain.

She resisted going into trance every step of the way but in that resistance we found humor and that was one way to begin healing. We prayed:

Not me, not me

and waved white silk flags of surrender to life the way it had been and prayer flags of brilliant colors to beckon her forward.

This may sound terribly odd, but it worked. She looked forward to her sessions, as I did, and her pain dramatically lessened. Last I heard she had returned to work part-time and her walking had improved enough for her to do errands without pain. This, she said, made her grateful and she found she could adjust to some disability now that she had some of her normal life back. And gratefulness in her prayers made her a happier person.

Practice: A Prayer for Physical Health

Begin to collect a list of words to describe your health situation such as *needles and pins, crawling around, shooting*. Now write awhile about what these words mean to you from your past experiences. See if you can develop a prayer from these meanings.

Larry Dossey was a battalion surgeon in Vietnam, chief of staff at Medical City Dallas Hospital, and is the author of *Alternative Therapies in Healthcare and Medicine,* and *Healing Beyond the Body.* He is a tireless advocate of the healing mysteries of prayer. He writes, "I propose a new variety of medicine I want to call eternity medicine. This is contrasted with what could be temporal medicine, which assumes that birth and death are the absolute beginning and end of life. Eternity medicine recognizes that some quality about us isn't confined to the flowing river of time, and that immortality and eternality are givens."

We are always moving, sometimes slowly, sometimes quickly, always somewhere undetermined. It is prayer that can offer us a harbor in the fast changing paces of life. Prayer offers us a power to walk in the light of what is and what is to become. It can give us courage to heal and understand that whatever life situation is given, we will be able to cope with the situation: not just survive, but thrive with humor.

> *I am the child of spirit. I live in a harbor of the spirit of things.*

We know that if we put ourselves in the way of danger, we may find it. If we lay down our bodies in the path of love, we will have a better chance to feel love, whether it is fleeting or lasting. We feel the night as hard as coal or as the holder of potential warmth. We can sleep on the pillows of hope or with the heavy wool blankets of despair. We can point ourselves in the direction of that what we want and surrender:

> *All in its order. I work, I pray, I accept.*

Author George Eliot in *The Mill on the Floss* writes about longing: "It seems to me we can never give up longing and wishing while we are thoroughly alive. There are certain things we feel to be beautiful and good, and we must hunger after them."

In prayers of possibility, we ask to feel our authentic selves, which are often buried under our alienated selves. It is in and through relationships, through healing our broken relations with our bodies, and with other people, that we might find the spirit that lives in all things.

Practice: A Path of Golden Light

Imagine a prayer that would put you on a path of golden light. If there is a sick person in your life about whom you are concerned, put her/him on the path. Hold the image and pray.

PART THREE

*

Prayers for Living Your Dreams

I am a leaf in bright color, free and ready to do its season.

In a wonderful book, *The Winged Serpent* by Margot Astrov, I found the fullest description of native American prayer I have seen, complete with background of meaning and sections of prayers. What was most interesting to me was that *the word* (chant, prayer) is considered most important to the indigenous people. It is believed that it is the thought, the dream, the word, that called life into being.

Song was used as an important way of communicating but melody itself had no meaning; it was used only to strengthen the magic power of the word to influence and bring about change. "The word, indeed, is power," writes Astrov, "It is life, substance, reality. The word lived before earth, sun, or moon came into existence. Whenever the Indian ponders over the mystery of origin, he shows a tendency to ascribe the word a creative power all its own. The word is conceived of as an *independent entity*, superior even to the gods."

Where prayers of possibility call for what we desire, prayers for living our dreams begin to give a more solid direction to this call. In order to pray for our dreams to come true, we need to create a vision of what comes next and be mature enough to follow through with our vision. Native Indians believe that prayer engenders just such clarifying of action; word gives power for humans to use in change.

I stand with lion and bear under the sun. I am animal. I drink
from the mountain spring. I am the mountain. I am the spring.
I sit, dance, hunt, and eat. I am the arrow that finds my mark.

And so we turn to these prayers for living our dreams.

CHAPTER 11

ᕀ

Prayers for Moving into the Unknown

Living your life believing in the mysteries, knowing, for instance, that the mist you see in the morning is fairies dancing at dawn, makes life an adventure. Believing only in facts, that condensation creates the mist and the fog, puts a heavy wear on the sole of your shoe. Better to look to the clouds forming hopping kangaroos across the sky asking you to come closer.

The native Americans had song prayers that helped in their growing up and in their survival. The Indians of the plains had their young males move beyond their troubled teens to go out into solitude to seek a vision in which the great Wakonda may show himself and give the youth a prayer song to use all his life. The youth fasted and took this long vigil asking for supernatural help, which may or may not have been granted.

The young women of the Chiricahua tribe in the deserts of the southwest were led in a puberty ceremony that lasted four days and ended at sunrise on the fifth day. The girls were offered blessings and songs for long life. Here is part of a prayer from *The Winged Serpent*. It is credited to George A. Dorsey's *The Tradition of the Caddo*:

I come to White Painted Woman,
By means of long life I come to her.
I come to her by means of blessings.
I come to her by means of her good fortune.
I come to her by means of all her different fruits.
By means of the long life she bestows, I come to her.
By means of this holy truth she goes about.

You have started out on the good earth:
You have started with good moccasins:
With moccasin strings of the rainbow, you have started out.
With moccasin strings of the sun rays, you have started out.
In the midst of plenty you have started out.

A chant for the young today might be:

You were welcomed to us as a beloved child and now you
have grown.
You are strong and have learned much,
active and moving as the mountain streams,
changeable as the air over water.
We wish you long life.
We wish you love.
We wish you wisdom to ask for help and to learn more
every year.
We give to you the world
we have helped make
and ask you to be a shapemaker of tomorrow.
We ask you to know you are human, a part of all things.
We ask you to know you are human, a part of us all.

Practice: A Song for Yourself

Write a song for yourself as you imagine yourself in a passageway, a time of possibility. Start with:

You, there, changing woman ...

Whether we mature through ritual or duties, a part of maturing is coming to terms with moderate thinking and leaving behind such extremes as always and never, excess and perfection in favor of being human beings living not in black and white but in all the colors of the rainbow connected to each other.

Essayist Anne Lamott talks about perfection: "Perfection is the voice of the oppressor, the enemy of the people. It will keep you cramped and insane your whole life." We pray to give ourselves time and encouragement to learn all that we need to know. We know that life isn't easy even when we work hard and we let ourselves stumble and fall and start in again, learning our lessons and gaining in experience.

Rosalind Russell, an actress of the Forties famous for her direct speaking style, is quoted as saying, "Flops are part of life's menu and I'm never a girl to miss out on a course."

I remember all the times I have gone belly up and seemingly failed to hold a job successfully or mother well or write the book the editor wanted. All of it was difficult at the time. Yet, none of it mattered really for, in the whole of things, I have done well.

The spirit didn't promise me to be the best. She said she would hold my hand and stay connected to me as I made mistakes, corrected them, and remade them, until grace came and I changed or I was led down a different path.

Let it happen,
a woman changed into grace.

"Real strength comes from knowing we can survive," Carole Hyatt and Linda Gottlief reassure us in *When Smart People Fail.* They talk about rebuilding ourselves for success and how the gift of failure is to stretch us beyond our conscious capacity so that we can grow into our authentic selves."

I remember once hearing a panel of the most famous and dearly loved of the feminist crones, including Gloria Steinem, Betty Freidan, and Bella Abzug, ask themselves what it is they had learned now that they were all over sixty. The consensus was that each had been through life's fire in her own way and survived, and not only survived but with humor, thrived. It is this knowing that you will bob up again even when hitting the ocean's floor. And humor, no small thing.

I could agree with this from my life. Nothing has killed me yet and I still have high spirits and the curiosity to explore and desire to adventure beyond what I know.

Gail Sheehy, in one of my favorite books, *Passages,* also talks about what is learned by middle age if we have used our years to become wise. For the fireworks of love, she says, "We learn that fireworks pass and are not worth a great change in themselves; the same three essentials stay the same: trust, care, and commitment."

I pray for sparklers and
the gentle calm.

Sheehy goes on to say, "Having experimented with many techniques for facing problems and change, they (wise middle-aged) will have modified many of the assumptions and illusions of youth. They are practiced. They know what works. They can make decisions with a welcome economy of action." It is this we hope will be shared with youth as parents, teachers, therapists and counselors, politicians, and spiritual persons. We can show our youth that after experience is incorporated by seeing and feeling into the person, sometimes directions become apparent if one is to be a successful human. It is with an attitude of sharing and not protecting your own inflexible position that others can hear:

My experience, my journey of hope and healing.

Practice: A Prayer for a Peaceful Life

Name five things you have learned by experience that helps you live a more peaceful life. Make these into a prayer.

We find that institutionalized religion gives us comfort when we don't ask too many questions and don't take our experiences into account. When we move beyond conforming to questioning, we find ourselves in a transpersonal state from which spirituality is born, for spirituality asks what is it that fosters our growth and happiness and how meaning be found in the days of our lives.

Practice: Finding Your Soul's Desire

- Pray for guidance *(Wise Woman, lead me to freedom)*, then write in your journal, using the method of dialoguing between your wise person self and your confused self.
- Visualize letting go of unnecessary things and then of feelings and cravings.
- Image yourself free to be yourself and visualize yourself walking, talking, and being free. See what activity you are drawn to.

We don't know what the future will bring but we do have an idea that the preceding practice will make your life happier. As William A. Barry writes: "There is no guarantee God will act in a certain way toward someone trying to live a good life. One plants one's feet firmly in midair and marches on faith, hope, and trust. The only verification we get is continued peace and joy on the journey."

✼

CHAPTER 12

Freeing Your Imagination

Imagination is the highest kite that can fly.

LAUREN BACALL, ACTRESS

The imagination is one of the best tools we have for creating prayers for the living of our dreams. All you need is the belief that your imagination will help your life and it will be so. With this belief, you will find yourself leaning toward imagination in problem-solving and in discovering what you value and it will show its wonders of new options and creative ways.

You begin to realize that all that you can imagine you can achieve, for *imagination is more than escape and idle daydreaming but a way to rehearse what you can help come alive.* Whether we are conscious of it or not, it seems that all great deeds start in the imagination and are put into the world, often at first by a courageous few, by those who believe the living of their dreams.

Think of the civil rights movement where black folks began to envision a total freedom including sitting on a bus wherever there was a free seat. Rosa Parks made the media splash but there were others at this time who refused to give up their seats to white folks.

Small deeds are sometimes enough to change our life. One client found that just by stopping herself from slamming the door with a *no way* attitude and instead letting the door stay ajar to new solutions, her mind would conjure up helpful ideas.

I changed by remembering.

A friend found she could not continue nursing because all she wanted to do was make quilts and weave. She took an early retirement and her house is now filled with quilts. She told me last night that she has happiness but a new problem: money.

We brainstormed ways she could work part-time until she is ready to sell her artwork at craft fairs. She realized she could imagine herself working on a contract basis, giving flu shots or something, and then having months to herself before she picked up another contract. Though it was initially hard for her to open her imagination wide and think outside the box, she realized that this she could do, and it would give her life a wonderful rhythm.

Let imagination better my life.

When I was young and in difficult circumstances I always thought that imagination did more than enrich my life. I used creating stories and building forts and making paintings to connect to my muse. Imagination never felt like a luxury to me but an essential way of both coping and putting happiness into life. I can only imagine the extent of loneliness I would have felt if I had not relied on the muse to bring connection through poetry. It is through imagination that I became comfortable with prayer because I knew that much good of life was unseen but felt in the bones.

Practice: Letting Your Imagination Fill Your Prayers

Imagine a world of cooperation rather than competition. Imagine people seen as equal and not one up or one down in status to others. Imagine the feeling as you walked the streets or lived in a house with others.

In fact it is our imaginations that may very well save the world. We know that power and money can control but cannot solve the ills of the world. New leadership needs to come about that includes thinking outside of the box and using imaginative thinking to solve humanity's problems. *Let us imagine together.*

We need leaders who are calmly able to endure not knowing all the answers but secure enough to know that the road ahead is new; leaders who will bring imaginative thinking along with knowledge, experience, and courage to take risk for the good of all. Leaders who are content to solve one problem and know that the path is unclear and uncertain and yet feel balanced and secure in their lives to meet the unknown. Leaders who know that prayer to the spirit of things is not necessarily religious but necessary.

American writer Nancy Hale writes in *Adventures of the Mind*, "Imagination is new reality in the process of being created. It represents the part of the existing order that can still grow." We need to recognize what good we can keep and what we need to heal. Each of us living regular lives can have a great part in our times by taking issues to prayer and being willing to sit quietly not knowing but with a willingness to seek the questions to ask and to hear the answers.

I went to a Women for Peace celebration, for a 9/11 anniversary, and on the stage were the Women in Black who, since 1979, have been standing weekly vigil on street corners in major cities around the world, asking for peace. Many of the women on the stage were grandmothers. There was much talk about "grandmother" wisdom and using this wisdom to find solutions. Grandmothers who have come to a time in their life where reflection and prayer and the use of imagination holds a vision of hope.

Prayer asks us to have faith. Another way to say this is to imagine the spirit until the spirit is felt in the feelings and body. Women have long been saying there are many ways to "see" and faith is one way to endure hardships in life, to know that with all of life's tragedies there are also surprises of startling joy. When we have faith in prayer, we know that we will continue to go along the windy path that is our life and be alright.

We pray for transformation of what is in our control.

⚘

CHAPTER 13

Signposts: The Symbols of Life

Another tool we can use in prayers for living of our dreams is a belief in the symbolic life. Much as the central African Hadgoe tribe uses an indicator bird to find where the honey is, we can search for meaning in the symbols all around us.

The symbolic and imaginative lives overlap and enrich us. For instance, in the forest of France and the making of cognac, the first vapors that steam off are called the *portion for angels* or *l'angles portion*. Without imagination or seeing the symbolic in the steaming off process, we could say the first vapors are not used and just disappear into the air. But, to give the vapors to the angels as an offering, puts meaning into every part of the process.

It reminds me of the writing process. I tell my students that often the first lines of a poem or story are the liftoff, useful for getting us to the place where the poem takes a drive. We couldn't do without that start, that push, that launch. We then start after the takeoff, where the language is strongest, where the imagination comes in and symbolically we are kicked into action. Writing lines come from the help of our portion for angels.

Symbols can be seen everywhere. We might see the flickering holiday lights as a symbolic reminder of our unsteady willpower that needs a spirit's hand for serenity. We might feel the love and warmth of a small dog indicates that love is everywhere, or that the warm breeze reminds us that change is coming. We allow the symbolic world to give us another level of experience; this paying attention to spiritual indicators allows us to be praying all day long.

I can see. Help me see.

We allow this awareness to affect our teaching, our business, and our writing. We push the broom with love and drive our cars in the long stripe of commute, aware of a plan designed to carry us to work; we accept the weave of our logical, conscious life and dreaming, subconscious life. We take this awareness to prayer and make a simple altar in the corner of our bedroom which at a glance reminds us that there is prayer in the world. We put a symbol of our love in the form of a photograph of our loved one. We put a sprig of evergreen on the altar to symbolize life eternal. A small shiny marble reminds us of innocence and children and those we want protected.

I have always enjoyed knowing the symbolism in nature and wrote a book of essays about the symbolic physical world, *The Wise Earth Speaks to Your Spirit*. My life is enriched when I see a bird and think of the bird as a messenger from my spirit. I like knowing the *onion* symbolizes revelation and *salt* immortality. Symbols help me better connect to the natural world by "close-seeing" and playing with deeper meanings.

Moon, shaper of change and renewal, hear our prayer.
Sun, the center and heart of the sky, feel our heart.
Tree of life, for us, for me.
Pear, round and healthy, great health and hope.
Desert, twin of desolation and contemplation, hold life bright.

We use symbols such as an arrow through a heart to show Valentine's Day. We sketch a halo over a person's head and we all know we mean he is holy or, at least, acting that way. Symbols carry deeper meanings and can help us cultivate prayer by externalizing the internal prayer and that can be important.

My heart to the heart of the world.

A troubled young friend uses a cross to symbolize balance and his prayer life even though he wasn't raised in a Christian church. He guesses that the symbol comes from the culture and it relaxes him. He uses doodling to let go a bit and says doodling is his form of prayer because as he doodles lines and circles, strings of thoughts come to him sounding like prayer.

Help me believe.
Tie my life with meaning.
Let me find a way.

I once had a vision come of living by water with a symbol of a creek behind a small cottage. Up until then I hadn't thought of living by water much although my happiest times were swimming in the lakes and rivers abundant throughout Ohio. I'm not sure how it started – in my writing, in my daydreams, but I saw myself taking a "water walk" each morning. I'd see it in my dreams and it would come up in my writing. It felt very strong but very far away.

Years later I moved to California and lived on a marsh with the Corte Madera creek winding its way past my back door to the Pacific Ocean. The symbol had come true but I had the lease of the place only for a time of transition, and I left loving my time there but somewhat disappointed that I couldn't stay.

More years have gone by and now I live on the mud flats of the San Francisco Bay watching the tide go in and out. It wasn't until I was walking one morning that I remembered the vision of the morning walk near water. Suddenly, it flashed that I was living where I was supposed to live. I almost missed it because the bay was on the right side and in my vision it was on the left, and the original symbol was a river, not a bay. Just then I realized that I take the form of things too seriously and don't notice what I am given. Now, when I get out my walking shoes I thank and respect the symbols that come to me and feel especially at home here.

If I had been more alert, I might have gotten to the water's edge sooner. Prayers for living my dreams might have made it more purposeful. As it was, I was both aware and unaware of the power of symbols, and I was given a gift embedded in my heart's prayer for water.

This is the kind of change that comes on tiptoes and leaves its marks on us. South African author Nadine Gordimer in *The Lying Days* writes of this:

"It is not the conscious changes made in the lives by men and women – a new job, a new town, a divorce – which really shape them, like the chapter headings in a biography, but a long, slow mutation of emotion, hidden, all-penetrative; something by which they may be so taken up that the practical outward changes of their lives in the world, noted with surprise, scandal or envy by others, pass almost unnoticed by themselves. This gives a shifting quality to the whole surface of life."

It is this shifting quality with which prayer life can help us, can provide a healing environment as we give ourselves time to change. Sometimes I think this is enough, just to be held until we can develop the part of us that is unhurt, compassionate.

Sometimes prayer gives us faith and a symbol with which to hold on. A young man I know, Stan, used to work for a company that tested water purification systems; he was frequently on the road. What he really wanted was to live in the woods and so he prayed for it with all his heart. In his prayers he kept seeing himself in a tree house, happily looking out on a forested vista. This image didn't make logical sense but it was so strong he just continued to believe in it.

Finally, he checked into jobs with the park service and found one for which he qualified. He said he would have just daydreamed about this except the symbol kept coming to him in prayer, which made it feel real. It gave him faith to take the leap. He kept praying to get clear about economics and his values before he could make a home at the edge of the forest he loved, and the tree house helped him stay on track. That's what trusting in the symbolic life can do for us.

In his book *Spirits of the Earth*, Bobby Lake-Thom writes,

"The concepts and symbols inherent in Native myths and Nature stories are located in and operate out of the subconscious part of the mind. This is the home of ancient and natural symbols, creative imagination, intuition, psychic powers, dreams, and visions. This is the space in our mind-brain complex where concepts, reality, and such phenomena as invisible playmates, spirits, talking animals can be positive or negative, masculine or feminine, physical or spiritual. They all have a purpose, function, and meaning in terms of developing our intelligence, human potential, and spirituality."

Practice: Learning from Your Spirit

Imagine a spirit that lives your life with you. Is it a he or a she or beyond gender? Is it an ally to help you or a resource to turn to for comfort? Is there guidance in your spirit? Must your body be in a certain "space" to allow the spirit's effect? What can you learn from your spirit?

Is there a symbol you could keep on your dresser to remind you of your spirit such as a special stone or shiny object? Would keeping a candle there and lighting it every night be the symbol that you need to remember you are not alone? How could you pray with the help of your symbol? How would a symbol strengthen your prayer life?

At a recently adopted baby's welcoming, twenty friends were brought together by the adopted parents and, after blessings were spoken to the child, Nina, each of us put a flower on the altar and said a blessing or good wish. The symbol of the flowers created a lovely vision of the child's future and made everyone feel connected to her future and each other.

Bobby Lake-Thom continues:

"Symbols have power and meaning. Think about the circle for a moment. It has no beginning, it has no end; it is infinite. This is why we say it is sacred and holy. All of Creation is a great circle, our Universe is in a circle, life is in a circle, our sacred sweat lodges are in a circle, the medicine wheel is in a circle, most drums are shaped like a circle; the tepee and ceremonial lodges are circles, and we even hold council in circles because to hold a meeting in this way serves to dissolve potential conflicts and promote harmony. The symbol and power of the circle creates and promotes unity and wholeness."

I pray:

We are life without end, like the circle everlasting.

A simple circle. We are helped by this deep symbolic shape every day. By bringing symbols into awareness consciously, we can find ourselves feeling so much more grounded and connected to the past.

And taking symbols into our prayers can help us feel joined to our life.

I am all these:
the china hand that feeds me, the long-legged bird
that waddles her way through the mud flats,
the shore bird in her white dress that comes to find
warmth in the harbor.
I am the book whose pages hold knowledge,
the poem that holds the pulse of the heart,
wisdom in the shape of a tiny bell.

꙳

CHAPTER 14

Mining the World of Dreams

In forming a bridge between body and mind, dreams may be used as a springboard from which we can leap to new realms of experience lying outside our normal state of consciousness and enlarge vision not only of ourselves but also of the universe in which we live.

ANN FARADY, DREAM POWER

Leslie Spier has studied the dream world and the use of dreams in the native American culture and recounts this finding: "At the heart of the Maricopa culture was the dream experience. It was the one thing of which they constantly talked, the significant aspect of their life as they saw it ... Dream experience was the bottom of all success in life, and as such their constant preoccupation. Learning was displaced by dreaming ..."

When we work with our dreams we are saying we believe that life is bigger than what we see and can know rationally. I remember a very powerful dream where I was flying above a huge waterfall more powerful than Niagara Falls – a power that is all encompassing. It was as if the dream were a video and the camera at first hovered at the top of the falls, then went over the falls in a plunging fall, and returned to the top, where you could see the river and land behind the falls stretching far beyond what the eye could see. Then, it was over the falls again and you could feel the drop and spread out to the river and the land beyond. It was a feeling of enormity, of space and land and water and vastness beyond my wildest dreams.

Immediately, upon awakening, I knew that I had been looking at life with a tiny sliver of a view and that the dream was showing me the vastness of options and experiences that were mine to choose from. The waterfall seemed to represent the power of life to experience and change and, although I felt frightened, there was no harm done to me in the dream. From that dream I drew the courage to change my work life and even today when I think of it I realize that I need a bigger box for my thinking.

Practice: Discover What Is Being Voiced in Your Dreams

Working with dreams gives us a more holistic perspective and understanding of life, which in turn usually creates more balance. There's a technique I like to use, where you write down a dream and then think about what part of you is being voiced by each person or item in the dream. If you have trouble understanding a particular part of the dream, you can then ask that dream person or item to give you a gift and let yourself drift into your imagination and see what is given and what the symbol might be.

Here's an example of how you can use your imagination and discover the meaning behind the symbolism in a dream. Once I dreamed I was in a hole digging with my brother who was the eternal digger of my childhood. After waking and thinking about the dream, I asked my dream brother what I was doing and he said I was taking care of him. I asked the shovel what I was doing and the shovel said that I was strong and powerful. I asked the hole what I was doing and it said that I was using my power to focus on others, and I needed to dig deeper to understand my needs. From there, I composed this prayer.

In the earth, the answers.
In the earth, the prayer.
I pray to know my true nature.
I pray to know my ground.

Arising from the core of our psyche, dreams carry messages both practical and spiritual in nature. Carl Jung said we dream in universal archetypes that can help us decode our dream messages. For instance, when we dream of flooding it can help us better understand the dream to know that water is an archetypal symbol of change. The ancients said that dreams are spirit messages and they often used dreams to guide their way. If a medicine man or woman dreamt of flooding, he or she would counsel and prepare for change.

Practice: Dream Ritual

Here is a prayer ritual for dreaming that is common to many native traditions. First, take the smoke of lit sage and cedar and fill the air around you (smudge). You can usually buy these herbs at a health food store. Sage and cedar are believed to eliminate negative energy in the mind and set the stage for purification or dream entry. Sweet grass is then placed in the bedroom (or other sleeping space) to attract good forces. Choose some classical or new-age music that is soothing and play it before going to sleep. Choose a power object such as a feather or a shell and hold it for a few moments, praying to your spirit to remember your dreams and the messages they bring and allow yourself to fall to sleep coated in the power of the dream ritual.

I like to do a variation on this ritual where I focus my mind on the image of the pearl from the following Helen Keller quote: *"Once in a dream I held in my hand a pearl ... as I gazed into its shimmering depths, my soul was flooded with an ecstasy of tenderness."* I open my hands turned upward on my lap and instead of using a power object I see the image of the pearl. This is especially useful when I am traveling and do not have all my sacred objects with me.

From here we can make a prayer of transformation.

Let wisdom start here with the shimmering pearl.

I know that when I receive messages from dreams, I am much more likely to take guidance from them and bring them to my prayers than to believe in my conscious mind and willpower. In AD 400, Synesius of Cyrene wrote: "How often does a dream not prize the reality of dream events beyond that of waking experience?"

Once I dreamt of digging eighty feet through the mud to make a basement, to find the roots of life and make honey. From that dream I went about looking for the sweetness in my life. With simple phrases I would pray:

How soft the rain falls as it creates life and fills the waters.

I trusted the symbol of finding honey, partly because in dreaming I could actually taste the sweetness, which made it feel all the more "real."

One precaution about working with dreams: Last week, after I had done some research on prayer and its help in healing physical illness, I had a funny dream. I dreamt I was at the scene of an automobile accident just as the paramedics were arriving. It was a scene of crisis with lights flashing and hurt people. A medic grabbed his leather medical bag and, before helping the injured person on the ground, said to me, "The name of your book is *Medic Alert.*"

Remembering the dream in the morning, I laughed. Clearly this was not literally about the book; I took it as a reminder to switch my healthcare HMO, an action I had been putting off for a year.

My point is, use your good sense when following your dream symbolism. The symbolism should seem like a *good* idea to you and in the best interest of everyone. I suppose it's possible that

Medic Alert will play a part in my life that I don't know of yet, but it's more likely that the dream was in part a message that prayer is really important for good health. At any rate, I'm glad I moved on my HMO.

Cultivating Your Dream Life

Some clients say they just don't remember their dreams. I remember my dreams best when I am feeling connected to my spirit and my body. For me, this means enough down-time after work. I need to take time to process the day by being alone some. I find light housework helpful in transitioning from work to rest. Reading in bed before sleep also helps. An occasional prayer ritual helps as does asking to remember my dreams as I fall off to sleep. Not drinking or taking drugs helps, too, of course. I've had clients who use their alarms as a dream aid. They find that waking suddenly often helps them remember their dreams and keep a journal or tape recorder ready to record them the moment they wake up.

Dreams can be a rich source of prayer material and can be the content for a transformation. A client of mine was suffering from a depression and needed to get back into the swing of things. She dreamt of ice skating in an old-fashioned bustled skirt. She took the bustled skirt into her prayers, literal as it was, and asked for her energy to transform.

Let me be in the bustle of everyday.

Don't Forget Your Daydreams

And then there are our daydreams. We tend to think of daydreaming as "spacing out," but throughout history people have prayed their daydreams and in so doing encouraged them to come alive. By focusing us, prayer can help make dreams come true. Think about it: If you set a goal, work for it, and pray, and you reach your goal, who knows which of the three makes it happen?

I daydreamed for years on a life where I was doing creative projects to earn my living and now I'm an author of several books and also work creativity with people in individual counseling sessions and teaching. I followed my daydreams by praying, taking a chance on the vision, and learning to deal with financial insecurity. I did what it took and then put transformation of my life in the hands of prayer and the spirit.

Using your daydreams to help you find your way, you may want to tap into the rich ore of the past and discover what the vein of happiness was for you and bring it back to your life. Maybe it was the music in your home that was beautiful and now when you hear the close harmonies of a barbershop quartet you are returned to those early feelings of joy.

We can choose to daydream on purpose and discover great riches about ourselves, our lives, our need for transformation. We can take our daydreams to prayer and footwork and make them come true. For example, you may find yourself dreaming about owning an island and living there work free. Such a daydream could seem like a total fantasy or it could tell you that you need rest and time to yourself and you could start praying and working to get that rest.

Resting for now, enough to do.

What are the changing forms of your daydreams? Keep tabs on yourself. Once you may have been dreaming of winning the lottery but now you are dreaming of working in sales so you can be out and about and meeting people. Your prayers might be full of movement.

I want to breathe fresh air.

In prayers for living our dreams we admit we are human with strengths and weaknesses and offer ourselves as we are. We pray for transformation to be our best self and treat ourselves as new seeds as we continue on this journey of growth and change. It is the new seed of ourselves that we can hold as vision until we can embody the growth and flower. What is important to notice is that daydreams lead us to create a vision for our lives and this we can take to our prayers.

Practice: Opening to Spirit

Breathe into your belly, the gut of your body that gives you a life force. Now find a special place in the mind's eye, a place that you may have been to before or an imaginary place of ease. Let yourself smell any fragrances. Step into this place and feel the quiet and how good that feels to your body.

Let yourself enjoy a deep breath of relief and sink into the feeling of peace that your special place offers. Now stretch your arms open, hands open and cupped upward. You are open. Stay in this posture awhile and feel what it feels like to have your heart area and chest exposed.

You are open to your spirit. Your heart and chest are exposed. You are asking for spirit to find you and as you ask, spirit will come. Imagine the gentle presence as you relax and drop your open arms into your lap, hands open and upward. Yes, it is the presence of your spirit. The wise one who is with you and loves you. You are in spirit. You are held in the grace of spirit. Open-hearted, your spirit hears your call.

✿

CHAPTER 15

Creating A Vision

Let there be many windows to your soul ...
Not the narrow pane
Of one poor creed can catch the radiant rays
That shine from countless sources.

ELLA WHEELER WILCOX, "PROGRESS," FROM *POEMS OF PASSION*

I work with a client, Greta, who is in the process of forgiving herself for bullying her sister when they were kids. She has the awareness that she too was a child and that she didn't set up the competitive system (systems are always set up by the adults of the family), and that she was trying to get the little attention that was available. That was not bad in itself. That she lorded over someone was, however, harmful to both of them.

She wants to be free of this guilt and be better friends with her sister, but she is pushing the river by wanting her sister to forgive her. That is not her business. It is a continuation of bullying. Her sister will forgive her if and when she can.

In prayers for living our dreams I lead Greta to take awareness and deepen it with the grace of acceptance. She takes the truth as she knows it to prayer.

I am this person who bullies and who is sorry.
I don't really know how to stop.
Help me learn cooperation and understand that I am all things:
the bully, the underdog, the cooperative person.
Let me choose cooperation. Let me choose love.

In her prayer she says what she is doing and how she feels, *I am this person who bullies and who is sorry.* She tells where she is in the process of change, *I really don't know how to stop.* Then she asks for what she wants and tells any larger insight that might help her get what her heart longs for, *Help me learn cooperation and understand that I am all things: the bully and the cooperative person.* Finally, the transformation she wants, *Let me choose cooperation. Bless the neglected children, both of us.*

Greta may need to dig deeper by journaling to come to the insights that she can only be responsible for her behavior and that her sister will need to forgive according to her own insights. Journaling or talking to a trusted friend or therapist may be the way Greta understands she can only do so much. Her final prayer line might be: *Love to my sister, bless us both.*

With the help of prayer she may find herself better accepting herself and finding that her actions are not only in the mode of making up for past wrongs and asking for forgiveness but that she is also using prayer as a way to acting differently toward her sister.

Creating a bigger vision of ourselves starts with awareness of our patterns and acceptance that we have this concern and these feelings. We sit with these feelings knowing that they must be accepted. If we are sad, we must accept our sadness and take it to prayer.

Yes. Me.
All of me including this.

Continue this practice of prayer for acceptance. Follow this prayer action when you feel ready.

Practice: Prayer of Acceptance

Write this prayer down on an index card and put it in your pocket every day for a week. During the day, read the card and take a few minutes to breathe the prayer's message into your body.

Spirit, I offer myself to your care. Show me the way, allow me to follow a nature most deeply mine. Help me create a larger vision of myself.

Practice: Creating Prayers for Living of Your Dreams

1 Name something you are doing that you want to transform.
2 How do you feel about doing this? Where are you in the process of transformation?
3 What would you need to change?
4 What would you need to give up?
5 What could you substitute for what you gave up? How could you make that work?
6 What insight might help you transform? Write it out in

your journal. If you can't see what you might need to change, pray: Please grant me the willingness to see what I need to see.

7 From the insight, write a prayer. In the prayer be sure to have a prayer action to which you can commit. (See example below.)

Ruth wanted to become more assertive at her place of work. She hated it that she wouldn't stand up for herself. She could speak up when she trusted the boss but not when she felt the weight of his possible disapproval. She wanted to be a woman who was at ease with authority, speaking up, agreeing or not; she wanted to be free to be her most helpful self. It was the idea of being her most helpful self, actually, that transformed her passive pattern.

In her prayer action, she used the vision of being a useful person. She knew she was imaginative and smart. She was good with details, math, and analyzing data. She was also well-liked and was herself the kind of boss for whom people worked hard.

In her vision, Ruth saw herself achieving everyone's goals by using her own best talents and skills. She could feel herself wanting to be more of a team player. The insight *for the good of all* helped her.

This is the prayer exercise Ruth did:

1 Name something you are doing that you want to transform.

I act timid but now want to give my opinion even when I feel intimidated and fearful.

2   How do you feel about doing this? Where are you in the
    process of possibility?
    *I am fearful but determined to change. I know it's possible
    over time.*

3   What would you need to change?
    *I would need to change taking the easy way out and not provok-
    ing any kind of reaction to what I might have to say. I would have
    to be seen as someone with whom others would need to reckon.*

4   What would you need to give up?
    *Security. I might be involved in a conflict and would have to
    deal with feelings about that.*

5   What could you substitute for what you must give up? How
    could you make that work?
    *I would have to change from being seen as the nice girl to a
    woman who speaks her mind. I could make it work when I
    think of the self respect I would have for myself.*

6   What insight might help you transform?
    *I am losing the battle of being a good manager and effective
    leader and if I don't change, I could eventually lose my job.
    The insight of short-term pain for long-term gain helps here.*

7   From the insight, write a prayer.
    Insight: The time is now.
    *Prayer: The time is now. The time is right for me to speak
    up. I am a steady tree. I have roots. I stand firm. I say what
    I need to say. Breathe deep. The time is now.*

There are other times when we actually behave poorly and the situation demands that we apologize or confess. Often this confession is accompanied with a feeling of shame, a feeling that you are a bad person. Shame is such a tricky emotion: you can no longer distinguish that you are a good person who sometimes acts poorly.

With prayers for the living of our dreams, we can get out of that old framework of confession. We can ask ourselves to become aware of our feelings and accept that they are part of your humanness. Let's take jealousy. It may be a trait you don't want to feel but feel you do. But in awareness you choose not to hamper another person's growth by acting jealously and trying to restrict her choices.

This is an example of what the process for a prayer of transformation might look like as we search for our vision:

I can be a jealous person and limit my partner's friendships. I feel insecure even though John is trustworthy. I don't know how to let go of those feelings of insecurity although I'm feeling a little less jealous lately. I don't want John to limit his social life. I don't want to limit him in any way. Let me be released from these nagging doubts and worries and focus on the good between us. Commitment and freedom in our relationship will help us grow and stay happy together.

Your prayer:

Free and committed, continued happiness.

Again, it's human to have the feelings, but through prayer you can choose not to act on the feelings in the same old way.

Let me remind you that you are seeking through prayers of transformation a way to envision positive change in a troubled area, and one positive action is prayer itself. Your prayer practice will allow you to live in the spiritual center of action; it gives you a vision to say with your tongue, see in your imagination, feel in your heart, and read on the paper before you.

In prayers of transformation, we see a repeating pattern and want to address the pattern with a new vision. Prayers of transformation are issues thought through and worked with until a possible solution comes to our folded hands.

A few words about what we call a true calling, a feeling that comes with the sense that your heart's deepest desire is being fulfilled. The Quakers call it *leading*. "A true leading," writes Charlotte Fardelmann in *Nudged by the Spirit*, "touches a deep level in oneself. It resonates on the deepest level of our own desire."

In my experience, I didn't know writing was my true calling until I was into my second book and I had worked through the fear so that I could actually feel the *leading* that had followed me throughout my life unnoticed.

Calling a Circle of Allies

Remember too what Oprah Winfrey said, "*No one does it alone.*" If you haven't already done so, make a list of the people who might have information or insight on your present concern.

Ask them for information. Make a list of people who could just listen to you as you clarify your feelings. Call them. And, if your list isn't long enough, join a group and get to know more people.

There are a few things that help as I set a vision for myself. I often think of holding a dream in one hand and a hindrance in the other. I ask my prayers to help me concentrate on the dream and not the blockage. For instance, if I want to teach at a special health spa and hate the cold call, I concentrate on seeing myself at the spa teaching journal keeping and not on my fear of rejection:

Here I am. Happy and teaching.

I remember the commitment I made to my younger self that I would leave a record of which I could be proud, and might encourage others to try still more than I did. I didn't want to have it found out after my death that I could write. I wanted to take the chance in my lifetime. As I neared fifty, I took the chance and wrote, hoping that someone in their twenties would read my work and take her own risks; that in that way I could be a model for someone else. I hope so and that my story helps keep the world of vision going:

I wish for the best for all of us.

✳

CHAPTER 16

Saying "Yes!"

Opportunity, everywhere.

There are many stories out there of ordinary people who believed in a something and made it work. We love these stories: the worker with vision who becomes the musician he is by deciding to pick up his beloved clarinet during a layoff and find himself a job with a local band; the woman who does what she wanted to do twenty years ago and goes back to school to get a teaching credential; the housewife who writes and publishes articles about staying home and staying sane; another who finds she has a talent for constructing crossword puzzles and becomes the crossword puzzle editor for a large New York City newspaper and, at her retirement, makes it her mission to supply every hospital in New York with free puzzle books.

These stories in which ordinary people transform their lives give us hope. They tell us that so much is possible in this life. We can take that hope to our prayer life.

Turning Fear of Failure into Willingness to Risk

If you are having trouble actually believing you can transform your life, you may be locked into fear of failure. I understand. If the law of your family was that if you tried something, it was up to you to get out of it on your own, you will not be willing to risk much. Failure would loom too heavy on your weary shoulders.

Let's write a healthy family law of risk and support. It might be: The children and grown ups in our family have the right to try new things so we can learn and grow and have fun. The children might talk to the adults first and get feedback as to the danger or logic of their choice. The adults would be encouraging in the children's best interest. The adults would help prepare each other and the children to succeed. Someone would either be with us as we risked or ask about it when we got home. Our family would be on our side. They would be there for us hoping for the best. If something went wrong, we could discuss it and see what we could learn and we could decide our next step. Risking would be an adventure that we and our family would be curious about and something we could share.

If that seems like a pipe dream, find *nonblood* family who would do this with you. You only need one or two friends with whom to dream and dare.

Let's take an example of a third grader who wants to be the youngest representative to student council. He tells his teacher and his parents of his desire to be a candidate. His parents might add to his allowance to buy poster paper and magic markers. His dad might make light pencil lines so his child could print in a straight line and create a poster that can be read more easily. His mom might dig out some old tomato stakes from the garage for his signs. The child might practice his written speech to his mom while she irons.

They would all wish him luck the day of the campaign. The day of the vote, they would ask how it went. If he won, they would ask for the details and be pleased. If he lost, they would ask for the details but be very interested in listening to his feelings and sense of loss. They would let him feel his feelings and be kind. Dad might make a special effort to spend time with his son that evening.

When time had passed, they might sit down and talk about what might have happened and what could be done differently next time and congratulate him on his trying. The focus would be on the boy's trying and not on the outcome.

A version of this happened to me with my son when he ran for student council in the third grade and won without my knowing anything about it. He came to me one evening and said he was worried. He was the representative for student council and the youngest one. The whole story poured out. He couldn't keep up with the noon meetings because he couldn't understand everything and didn't write very fast. He thought the little girl Gretchen, who had also wanted the job but lost, would have been better after all and he wanted her to do it.

We talked about it and he didn't want to tell his teacher his problem and be helped; he didn't like it at all. We determined we would sleep on this a night or two. When we talked about it again, he still wanted to quit so I walked to school with him and told him I would stand there as he told his teacher. My son said student council was too much responsibility for a little boy and he didn't want to continue. The teacher put his hand on his shoulder and said, "I had no idea this was so hard for you. I am so proud of you for trying these past six months and I am so glad you came and told me. I have seen you trying very hard. You have made a certain young girl very happy today." I was extremely touched by Mr Garrett's kind response. I flashed him a smile and hugged my son whose face looked innocent and happy.

My son had done an act without a vision and although successful in winning, he didn't make himself happy. Yet he was validated for taking the risk and still felt like a capable person. He learned to pay attention to the job not just the fun of winning. And that sometimes we get in over our heads, and that's okay too.

I could have easily centered on why I knew nothing about this but that would have put the focus on me. I had to let go that he chose not to tell me about the whole process until there was a problem and perhaps better show him he could count on me to be there in any part of a situation. Maybe he needed to know he could do it on his own or maybe he needed to better learn I would help him but that was not the issue he brought to me at that time, and I needed to respect that. Perhaps in helping him in the way he wanted would lead him to trust me more.

Support for our disappointments and failures is pretty much a fiction in many of our lives and so we heal our shame through prayers of transformation. In *Stirring the Waters: Writing to Find Your Spirit*, I wrote: "The spirit is us, lives with us, surrounds us, is deep inside us. And, we are still fine in our imperfections.

Remember, we are each everything at the same time: the healing and the healed, the doubter and the believer, the person of grace and the person who stumbles through the storm."

Practice: Writing New Laws of Family Support

- What was the script in your family about money, success, risk? Write out the law or script they followed. What was expected of your gender? How did they follow their own laws?
- How are you like and not like your family in this way? Go through each family and authority person and the gender law.
- How would you like to be? Who would be a good model for you either in your family or not. What do you like about this person's dealings?
- Apply this good model's behavior to your current situation. List some of the practical changes (your to-do list) you need to make, both those internal changes that take purpose and prayer and those that you will carry out in the world.
- Prioritize your list of practical changes and get started with action.
- Commit to doing one action a day.
- Finally, before bedtime be clear of what you have been asking to create with your prayers for the living of your dreams and be sure to name what you want and say in your prayer your insight and what you need to change.

Here's an example: Say you wanted to change your attitudes toward success. First your prayer would state that you wanted to transform your attitude toward success and also that you feel cautious because it had to be success in your value system and you aren't always sure what that value is until faced with it. You might say you are in the process of praying and journaling to become clearer about what you value. Then, as you look for a role model, you think of Eleanor Roosevelt. You decide to read more about her life and see how her example might inspire you to take action even when you are unsure.

I am becoming more and more myself.

Take time at the end of the week/month to re-evaluate all that you did concerning this issue. Your wise inner voice will let you know when you are on track. This can be done with silent prayer:

Guide me to my best self.
Let me say yes to possibilities.
Let me feel hope.

Recently I met with Beth, the guiding teacher of a Buddhist sanga of young people, and we talked about prayer. Beth told me she liked the first draft of this book but that she thinks prayer is a loaded word to many people and that meditation would be more neutral. We agreed that most of us haven't been hurt by someone's meditation practice while many of the Christian right prayers are said against women and minorities' rights to equality and freedom. She wondered if I could change the terminology.

We played with spontaneous expression, reflective or contemplative states, incantation. What words to reach people who needed to hear them?

An experience the next month changed her attitude a bit. Beth attended an outdoor wedding where everything was love: the grove, the circle of friends and family, the sweet smell of jasmine, the service of poem and song. In this setting, she felt a calling to prayer of the heart and thought about my book. She thought that maybe meditation was the call to be silent and authentically in the moment and prayer was the verse of the heart. Although she still had trouble with the word *prayer*, she felt that her practice was transformed to include prayer.

Beginning again, room for silence; room for dream.

Some time after the wedding we sat near the fireplace sipping tea, talking about how we change and how long it takes for change to come, how fast change comes.

Religious scholar Diana Eck writes in *A New Religious America*, "Muslims speak not just of praying every day but of 'establishing' prayer as a part of everyday life. In Islamic understanding, our human condition is not so much a matter of original sin but of perpetual forgetfulness. They combine church and state and weave prayer into the everyday."

Even in the United States, where we believe that the separation of church and state better allows us to be a diverse religious nation that also makes room for the nonreligious, we can pray from our hearts for transformation and enter a daily rhythm of prayer.

Living With the Mysteries

꙳

Praying to live your dreams is complicated in our complex society and we are asked to do our footwork and, at the same time, to access the power of the unseen. A wonderful attitude to develop, which will help you in prayers of transformation, is to fall in love with the mysteries of life.

If you want to travel for your job, you might envision a future of being a bird or hold to a vision of flying on an aircraft and relaxing with a book, your suitcase stuffed with goods to sell or fabric with which to make art. You can collect feathers for your altar and create a vision, as you also build up your savings and check to see the policies that would allow you to take a year off.

So, then what? Then we also have to realize that we *don't* always know what is best. When we throw a coin into the fountain with a prayer, we have to be ready for the possibility that something *else* will happen instead. That is the mystery. How about a prayer that says, simply,

I am a ripple in the sea. I belong to the whole. Guide me.

Spirituality and prayer helps us connect with the mystery of life. We long to taste the mysteries and just to explore the unanswerable affirms our lives. Through our spiritual lives we learn that seeking itself is the thing of life and not what is sought. As we pray for rain, we become the rain; as we watch the workers press on to strip mine in West Virginia, we become the scarred earth.

> **Practice: Vision Turned to Possibility**
> What has not yet lived in your life? Describe it to a friend in detail. Now write step by step how it could happen and write a prayer asking for guidance in making this goal become a vision turned to possibility.

How wonderful to live seeking something we do not fully know: the lessons that the surf has to offer as the beginning of the shadowed evening approaches help us better see through the soft light of the end of day.

Albert Einstein states, "The most beautiful thing we can experience is the mysterious. It is the source of all true art and science. He to whom this emotion is a stranger, who can no longer pause to wonder and stand rapt in awe, is as good as dead: his eyes are closed." Today we bring this awe to our spirituality.

> *I ask for circles of healing, the heartbeat,*
> *the planet in the mantle of love.*

To ask yourself important questions makes a difference. A Buddhist friend told me for him prayer is asking and meditation is listening. I'm not sure I could sort it out so neatly but I hear what he is saying. Like him, I believe that both asking and listening are important parts of the process of exploring beyond everyday concerns so we can find a place of transformation in ourselves.

We can ask to join into the quality of the mind that is not localized to individual brain and body, or even to specific

moments in time and space. I am reminded of a day at Green
Gulch Zen Center meditating outside. I was sitting on the
ground near a pond. The early spring brought the fresh smell of
the grasses and the sun was warm on my back. A red-winged
blackbird called out from time to time as it flew over the water.
I felt the hand of the spirit and I felt the whole of life surrounding
me. A perfect moment. Everything connected in spirit.

⚜

CHAPTER 17

Helping Prayer Work

One with you, One with you.

The hunters of the Eskimo tribes of the north lands believed it was *the word* that makes prayer work. They did not think women weaker than men simply because they did not go on the hunt. They knew that without the women, who stayed behind singing incantations to bring the game to the hunters, the hunters would return empty handed. To them, the song held the power of the hunt.

> *Oh Wakonda, on this land*
> *show me the way that I may*
> *become a brave man.*
>
> *Deer, we feel your spirit.*
> *Become one with us.*
> *Come with your heart to our heart.*

We don't need anyone to tell us how to pray because prayer is a natural instinct; it's feeling put into words. We remember or learn that wonderful body feeling of prayer or focused attention that is so deeply healing; the glorious feeling when we are in the moment and in that moment, nothing could be more perfect with the past faded into its place and the future resting on the shoulder of the spirit. You can learn to reach this place of focused attention simply by putting words to the song or the ache in your heart and calling it a prayer practice; in time, you will reach a place that satisfies you with connection to your spirit.

You might find yourself saying, *Please*, or *Thank you*, or *Help me*, or *Let me endure* or just repeat the words, *Oh, god*, or *Oh, spirit*. I recently found myself repeating, *One with you, one with you*. You might sit quietly with your eyes open or shut and repeat the words over and over until you can feel yourself calm.

It helps to believe that prayer works. If you find that you are fearful, you can send your prayer to the part of your body that signals the fearfulness, which is usually the breathing and a palpitating heart. Just sit and repeat what comes. *All fine in spirit. All fine in spirit,* until your heart calms. Just let the feeling be there and add your prayer and a belief in that prayer's power as in the words of Dutch resistance fighter, Corrie ten Boom in her book, *Not Good If Detached*: "You can do more than praying after you have prayed. You can never do more than prayer before you have prayed."

So, prayer works better if you believe it works and you also do your footwork. Once you have started your prayer practice you can start thinking about adding your possibility making steps in making dreams come true and in transforming your life much as we talked about in the last chapter of saying "Yes."

Rhoda told me that prayer helps her receive what she wants because once it's important enough to be in her prayers, she feels strongly, prays emotionally, and really works for her prayers to come true.

She had finally learned the truth of what Chuang Tzu, the great Taoist sage said in 360 BC: "*Use all your vital energy on external things and wear out your spirit.*" Rhoda had come to realize that the only way to stop her craving and attachments was to come home to herself. To her, this meant slowing down, having her days include exercise and prayer to focus her life on relationships rather than money and success. She found herself really believing that prayer could guide her. All she had to do was put the plan in action and prayer would show her if it was the correct decision for her if she would but watch and listen to both obstacles and ease.

What Rhoda wanted was to move to Houston. Her goal was to rejoin the loving community she had left for a career opportunity. As she prayed she could remember their warmth and the feeling of her chosen family. She put all her heart into that family! She felt love was a state of being and not outside but deep inside her. She prayed with love:

I'm coming to you as I come to myself.

She looked on the Internet for job openings. She talked to friends who lived in Houston. She networked with co-workers at her old job in Houston. She learned of an opening for which she qualified. She'd take the salary cut and go!

She believes her prayers *and* her actions worked together. She said every time she prayed she felt transformed into being a more loving person who had faith that this move for her good would happen. And so it did.

It never hurts to do our part. Often prayer is a matter of taking loving action for ourselves. Prayers steady us as we do one hard thing after another. They can be our guide.

Practice: Doing the Footwork

If you have something you are praying for, ask yourself at the end of the week, "Did I do the hard thing? Is there anything else I could do to help my pray work?" You may find yourself using extroverted skills that you didn't think possible. Do the footwork but let prayer be your companion with the spirit's touch surrounding you.

Stretching Beyond What We Think Possible

Our prayers are answered when they allow us to do what we need to do, perhaps are destined to do. They create a connection to our spirit that allows us to stretch beyond what we think possible. We do the hard things *because* there is a soft place of prayer.

Sometimes, of course, our prayers are answered even before the footwork begins. A client, Terry, was at the end of a messy divorce and her husband wanted to sell the house immediately. Moving and housing weren't her first concern. Her first concerns were getting over the breakup and stabilizing her income. She was angry and isolated. She prayed not to be an angry person; to take the lessons offered and move on.

> *Help me see my part.*
> *As I forgive myself, I forgive _____.*
> *As I forgive _____, I forgive myself.*

Her prayer gave her the strength to start talking about her situation, and just by talking to a family member she found a part-time nanny job, which supplemented her consulting income just enough to get her started. She felt cared about as she cared for children and not so isolated.

A very practical friend suggested that perhaps her husband could pay the losses on the house, which they had purchased just eight months before and had declined in value and maybe that would make the deal more fair for her. That reminded her to find out about her rights and she did.

She decided to get out of her bedroom and connect with others more. She remembered hearing about Alanon, the 12-Step group for loved ones of people with substance abuse problems, and in the spiritual discussion at the meeting she heard a woman talk about not knowing what to do, about staying in the not knowing and how courageous that was. She talked to another friend who told her about Affordable Living Apartments and she made an application. She started praying:

> **Let me know when I'm ready.**

She began the living of your dreams exercises I gave her and determined that she wanted to be a better person after this: more congruent with what she was doing and saying:

*Let me be a more accepting person. Let my anger be
considered. May I believe I am a good person. May I believe
I can take care of myself well. May I trust that I can be in a
caring community of friends.*

What she got out of this hurtful situation was the lesson that
she needed to be more honest with herself and also that it was
okay to be interdependent. Like most of us, she *needed* others.
Connection warmed with spirit.

I will know when I know.

Practice: Strengthening a Personal Quality
What personal quality could you identify that could use
some strengthening in you? How could this quality help
the living of your dreams? If you could touch this quality,
what would the texture be now? What would you like it
to be?

Remembering to Listen

Sometimes listening helps make our prayers work. The spirit
really does talk back to us. I once read a book on listening,
Soundscapes, by Bernie Krause, a bioacoustician, a man who
studies the sound of biology in the great outdoors. He believes
in listening for the joy of hearing nature and writes:

"Find a place that has no mechanical or other human noise and where there are only creature or natural sounds: a stream, a meadow, a lake, a favorite forest, a mountain, a beach, a marsh or park ... Give this effort enough time and you'll discover that there is a special aural fabric unique to each particular location ... Some sounds will be very subtle. Learn to listen to and discover your totem natural sounds – ones that especially draw your attention and resonate with something in your soul.

He calls these places the "natural wild." These, it seems to me, are the prayer sounds of the wild that are brought to us to help us transform by believing in the spirit alive in nature's sound and beauty.

Rabbi Steven Greenberg in the documentary *Trembling Before God* talks of using prayer as a salve or as an invitation to inquiry. Why shouldn't we sit with our spirit in *the natural wild*, open-minded, and ask to be led to clear thinking? Why shouldn't we trust that prayer with the spirit will bring good energy to an issue or to our lives? Why shouldn't we sit with the beauty of the world all around us and sink into the love of prayer?

Practice: Guided by Nature

Find a place in the natural wild, listening to the creatures of the forest or stream or meadow, and ask to be guided.

CHAPTER 18

⚜

Everyday a Source of Prayer

Lessons everywhere, and god.

Where do we turn to find our prayer words? What is the source of prayer? This is a place where people often get stuck. They say, "perhaps you can do this, but I just don't have the words. Where do I find the words?" We need only be aware of our present life to find our prayers. The everyday can be a walk of pilgrimage holding spirit in our awareness and moving toward the greater mysteries of god.

For instance, as I read some of the latest news of terrorism I saw a family named and chose to pray for them sitting on the patio facing the sun. As I felt the sun on my face, I said the simple words:

In the light, blessed be.

Another time I prayed as I sat eating my breakfast on the patio one morning, tiny bubbles floated down from the upstairs condo as the young boy who lives there played on his deck. I could have been annoyed but instead chose to notice how the bubbles brilliantly reflected the first sunlight of the day. Magic bubbles from the sky, I thought, and was transformed by the shower of these lovely circles of transparency.

Yet another. Straightening the house one morning, I noticed the greenery outside my window and was reminded of a Brazilian jungle I once visited. Thick, deep, a carpet for prayers. And so I started my prayer ritual that day by visualizing the oversized leaves from the jungle. Abundance! Here was a memory that I could always call on and know that I would have enough.

I made breakfast and by 8:30 a.m. I got to work on this book. As I sat down at my desk, I glanced over at the Barbara Kingsolver quote a friend had given me: "Praise incessantly, hold high expectations, laugh, sing out loud, celebrate without cease the good luck of getting set down here on a lively earth." Prayer.

Later in the day, as I did errands, I impulsively decided to stop at a new frame shop and asked them to cut two pieces of mat board, which I would use for collage. I hadn't done collage for years but I suddenly had an urge to make something with my hands. I'd been noticing a lot of Japanese woodcuts lately and they made me long to do art. I wanted to recreate some of my prayer feelings in pictures.

Practice: A Collage About Living a Dream

Gather materials: papers, magazine images, drawings, and glue and make a collage about the living out of a dream.

The day after making a collage and having time to reflect on it was a long one with hypnotherapy clients but no less spiritual. Being in the company of people searching to be themselves, realizing that the self is constantly reinventing itself and always under construction, is part of my spiritual practice.

Before starting my work day, I met my daughter-in-law at a coffee house and played with my eight-month-old grandson while she tutored a disabled teen. Matthew, just learning how to kiss, made a wet place on my face and then blew on it. That's how he thinks kissing is done! Then, we laughed together – me enjoying the new kind of kiss, and he at some pleasure it brought – and did he again and again. Love in innocence or innocence in love, he opens a deep spiritual place in me.

Bless this child. Hold him.

Wordless Prayer

We think of prayer as words, and it is, but it is also a way of being – holding an open heart. When a client tells me she hates herself for secretly judging others, she is expressing the feelings of a closed heart. I let her talk and see if my open-heartedness can affect her. I lead her to finding compassion for herself just as I am compassionate with her. I take the inner critic in her as a signal that she has lost touch with her own grace and spirit. I know that if we sit and "pray" by being open-hearted together, she will get back on track.

Let love heal.

Reading a story by Anne Lamott in last Sunday's paper where she talks about washing her dying friend's feet, I see this silent ritual as prayer in action. A meeting in love that changes lives.

My friend Shelia spent some time in her youth at a monastery south of Rochester, New York. "The spiritual experience for me was to be with the monks who spent much of the day chanting," Shelia says. Although she has never had much belief in a personal god, she did come to believe that there is some sort of guiding entity that is beyond human comprehension. "The Monastic experience showed me that I could feel something in the absence of understandable language. I didn't know the Latin in which they were chanting. I didn't want to know it because the music held me in awe. After that I've always thought that using language to reach the unreachable sets a kind of limitation on us. I pray without words, feeling only. Music to me answers what I need as my sacrifice on the altar."

Shelia does not want everything named. She reminds me of a quote by Tao Te, "A way can be a guide, but not a fixed path. Names can be given, but not permanent labels."

A client once told me of listening to the Bach B-minor Mass and *"in remissionem pecatorum,"* the contrapuntal development of the theme led into two or three tight places from which only a great musical mind could find exits. She sat in her room listening to the work of a genius. These magical moments inspired by music brought a prayer to her lips.

I believe.

An acquaintance of mine does chanting in Berkeley every Sunday night and finds chanting with community a way of prayer, a way to stop her chattering mind.

In *Praying with Our Hands* Jon M. Sweeney writes, "In Sufi dance, or 'turning,' the dervish becomes a doorway through which the Divine and human meet. Receiving energy from God with the right hand turned toward heaven, she returns energy to the earth through her left hand."

> *Draw me in your footsteps, let us run.*
> *The king has brought me into his rooms;*
> *You will be our joy and our gladness.*
> *We shall praise your love more than wine;*
> *How right it is to love you.*
>
> SONG OF SONGS, 1:4

Practice: Wordless Prayer
Decide on a kind of wordless prayer and do it today. It may be sitting with a symbol of an open heart (perhaps a lotus flower opening) or a sound or a turn of the body.

Walking Meditation

Another way of finding prayer in the every day is through walking meditation. I was introduced to walking meditation at the Hartford Street Zen Center in San Francisco. A small group of us sat and meditated and then we went out into the backyard summer garden and followed the stone path around the perimeter.

It was hard for me to slow down and yet I knew that prayer could be found if I could only be more deliberate with my body movement and concentrate. I tried to notice the details of the hollyhocks, the delicacy of the baby moss and purple violets. I noticed that the garden had much sun and that daisies and roses thrived side by side. Most of all I smelled jasmine.

Let me smell the sweet smell of flowers.

For me it was the smell that gave me the strongest sense of being there. I found that I could be with the garden in prayer, I could access spirit through my sense of smell. So I walked the path again noting the smell of the damp moss and white jasmine. Walking meditation to me was a reminder to follow my nose to the spirit that lives all around me.

Others find that just walking is a healing activity and can be prayerful. In *The Direct Path*, Andrew Harvey writes, "When researching aborigine culture, I discovered that for the aborigines, walking is the most sacred of all activities, the one they consider most naturally attuned to the rhythms of the cosmos and so rich with healing and calming properties." One day he saw Bede Griffiths – then in his mid-eighties – returning from a long morning walk down the riverbank near his ashram in South India; "his joy and balance seemed to radiate from the earth itself."

When Harvey asked Griffiths about his walking experience, Griffiths said, "I try to become one with the air and water and earth and with my breathing and I try and revel in the seamless dance my body and mind are doing with the world around me." He added, "Sometimes when I am really awake I really see that the trees are angels."

Practice: Touching Growing Things

Do a walk meditation focusing on spirit in everything you see. Give yourself permission to touch growing things.

Lessons Everywhere

Funny, I know, but I find going to the movies to be a kind of prayer. As I enter into another world, I listen and watch for those places in the story where families are finding the place in their woundedness to forgive and couples are finding the grace to concentrate on the good of each other. These, for me, are spiritual lessons.

For instance, in the film version of Jane Hamilton's *The Map of the World*, in which the protagonist's best friend's child has drowned in the friend's pond, I saw a portrait of how you can forgive a friend in time even when the hurt and sorrow may never go away. Some tragedies are just too big for the heart to handle although we live and survive past the tragedy. I watched the two women friends struggle with their friendship and thought of how deeply they valued each other. I understood *not* knowing how, not being able to figure things out. It reminded me of losses and unresolved relationships in my own life, and I prayed:

> *Let the best happen.*
> *Protect us.*
> *Let me be led.*
> *Watch over the deeply wounded in the world, please God,*
> *dear mother.*

I have even known a few people who cook with hands of prayer, especially those who cook together. Women have long known that to cook together and make bread together is a way of communion – with each other and their spirit. We share with each other; we share with a stranger. We make all welcome in the glowing heat of the kitchen, the heart of the house. As Thich Nhat Hanh says, "A piece of bread contains a cloud. Without a cloud, the wheat cannot grow. So when you eat a piece of bread, you eat the cloud, you eat the sunshine, you eat the minerals, time, space, everything."

For others, writing may become a source of prayer. My book *Stirring the Waters: Writing to Find Your Spirit* outlines ways to channel deeper in the heart of things and find peace. The journal is a way of witnessing our prayers and becoming more of ourselves. Here are some prayers from a client who wrote every day.

> *Let my walk be a dance on this earth.*
> *Let me follow a compass rather than a clock.*
> *Let me follow my spirit's hand.*

You might just stop for a minute and let out a prayer:

> *Thank you, spirit, for the peace of today in me and around me.*

You may sit for awhile with your eyes open, gazing at a lovely tree, and turn to a line of a poem for prayer, such as, *Only god can make a tree* or you may close your eyes asking:

> *How can I help?*

This Eskimo song could become your prayer:

> *The great sea has set me in motion.*
> *Set me adrift,*
> *And I move as a weed in the river.*
> *The arch of sky*
> *And mightiness of storms*
> *Encompasses me,*
> *And I am left*
> *Trembling with joy.*

Or a prayer you have written, such as,

> *Let good be everywhere – a waterfall – the fish flying their silver through it,*
> *the water before it and the water behind it,*
> *a gentle lapping near people who live with its cleansing and take life from its mouth.*

Practice: Everyday Sources of Prayer

List the things you love to do. How could your activities be an everyday source of prayer for you.

Poetry as Prayer

Because we are not bound by a particular tradition or text or set of prayers, we can use poetry as a source of prayer. Poetry points to the unknown with the vision of language and metaphor and helps us "see" the unknown. As African-American poet Audre Lorde writes:

> "Poetry is not a luxury. It is a vital necessity of our existence. It forms a quality of light within which we predict our hopes and dreams towards survival and change, first made into language, then into ideas, then into more tangible action."

You may not feel like a poet but everyone has poetry that lives in their body. You can write images and place them on a page and declare your words a "poem of the heart" which it is. Really, it is.

I didn't start writing poems until my late forties and found the presence of God on my own pages talking with me. Here is "New Horizons":

The sky opens and lightning runs the sky,
rain falls as tiny puffs on the leaf
of earth's wrinkled skin. This is heaven,
this round bubble of silence, my face
against this window. Never has there been
so much silence, such rest in deep corridors
of my body. How long I needed this.
When change comes to waken me,
it is cloaked
in speckled velvet, tiger fur, leopard skin.
These butterflies wave their wings
against the glass as if to ask me
to come back to earth,
live in the delicate storm of flesh again.

After writing this, I found myself repeating three prayers which were very helpful in keeping me on my path to rest and not becoming concerned about inaction in the world at this time.

I rest like the field – dormant, replenishing.
Silence is a song.
I'm held by life. Quietly, life lives inside of me.

I find the words of other poetry very helpful, I like the works of Mexican poet/activist Luis J. Rodriquez who writes very directly about urban experiences of the poor minority in LA. American Pulitzer prize winner and college instructor, Mary Oliver, writes well of the natural world and helps that world tie to your seeking spirit such as in the poem, "The Grasshopper," in which the final line asks: *And what will you do with your one wild and glorious life?*

Practice: Poems into Prayer
Go to the library and flip through poetry books until you find poems that touch your spirit. To what do you respond? Write down important lines to use as prayers.

I have a book from my childhood that my mother was kind enough to save for me, *110 Favorite Children's Poems*. It was through that book I learned about death in "Little Boy Blue" as the tin soldier stood on the shelf waiting for his master to return. I also learned about illness, love, and loneliness from the lines of those pages. It was the first time I realized melancholia and that I wasn't the only person lonely.

Today I look at the faded red cloth book cover and the binding that has come apart, the pages yellowed and crinkling, and remember the book I took to bed with me every night to learn about life and enjoy the verse. The poems triggered ideas in my forming mind and became my questions. Knowledge, beauty of language, inspiration, questions becoming prayer.

Let me know everything.
Let me feel everything.
Let me ride the pony down to the creek behind the barn.

I go to the Berkeley and Oakland library once a month and take out random books. I might take out a new book of poems such as the recently released book by Adrienne Rich, *Fox*, or an older book I haven't yet discovered, such as Quaker teacher Parker Palmer's book *The Active Life*. I read and learn and discard and believe what fits and in which I am ready to digest. I revisit the

Quaker church on Lake Street and enjoy the silence as we pray together. I return home and write about the spiritual power of silence and write a prayer:

Silence like snow holds.

I listen and find more reasons to write as a way of expressing what I learn from a life of spirit.

Sometimes my stack of library books includes books that I know I won't read all the way through but only peruse and enjoy sections that catch my interest. It's all prayer. Last week it was a photography book on the geography of the world's salt lakes and the beauty that can be seen there. I read the way hundreds of flamingos stand in line in Africa to drink the "poisoned" salt water and how only the flamingo, penguin, and pigeon regurgitates food for its babies in the world of birds. How penguins can hardly fly now since they so seldom do and I thought of how nature protects us and leads us in life down twisting and various paths.

Thank you for the world at my fingertips.
Mother, father, nature, room for all.

As you use your reading to discover your personal prayers, you might ask, Does this reflect my beliefs? Open new ways of thinking for me into which I want to step? Do I believe the message? Does it resonate to a part of me that I don't know about yet? Can I choose it in faith?

To deepen her spiritual connection, a friend of mine puts a book of quotations next to her bed and chooses a subject such as *rain* and reads "The smell of rain is rich with life," by Estela Portillo Trambley in *Pay the Criers*. She then spends a few moments in silence and writes down a prayer, such as this prayer of wonder and gratitude:

May I open my heart to the rich soil of my life.

Then, if she awakens to rain, she allows herself to enjoy the stormy day, remembering her prayer, and feels the bed of her life rich and growing.

So, use today as a source of spirit and don't wait for the soft bed of your two-week vacation to relax and feel more spiritual. Better to find a prayer practice in the everyday so happiness can live with you as a constant friend. And vacation? Well, that is wonderful too!

PART FOUR

❧

Tipping the Balance

To make a difference in this world of crazy ways, try being a carrier of kindness and let compassion show in your actions and words and hold all life as a prayer.

The idea of tipping the balance is to put more good into the world than there was before the dawn lit the day. We are a small piece of light that spreads over the land of our daily life so that no matter what is going on in the news, no matter what disastrous course our world leaders may be on, we have a part in gently tipping the course of the world to a better place.

All of us know what it's like to hear our negative voices talking up a storm, at least from time to time. With just a touch on my arm or a kind smile, we can be reminded that we are not our troubles but our gifts, and gifts are all around.

We can see every action we take toward making the world a more loving and compassionate place as a form of prayer and every prayer for peace as a form of activism. We can see every prayer we make for others as a way of tipping the balance toward the good and the green and the lovely; every form of activism in our lives as deeply spiritual. After all, why would we care to take the time or put our bodies in harm's way were it not out of great love and a deep sense of spirit. As we live a life of prayer we begin to understand that spirit is for all people in the human community. Just as we ask ourselves to find blessing, we ask that others are blessed.

CHAPTER 19

✿

Action As Prayer

It is when we're given choice that we sit with the gods
and design ourselves.

DOROTHY GILMAN, *CARAVAN*

The way I see it, prayer is the most radical peace action we can take because when we step into our heart of peace-making we create peace in ourselves and that's where it all starts. We leave behind our feelings of fear of what others might do to us and leave behind the feelings of being right or better. We simply pray that all men and woman are equal and worthy of consideration. We pray for a shared reality where there is enough for all. Any prayer from the heart that encourages acceptance and peace is a radical action.

You there, you are my sister.
You there, you are my brother.
You are my family and I bring you into my heart.
You are my family and I feel your heart.

Pema Chodron, in her book *Comfortable With Uncertainty*, writes about an inspirational practice in Buddhism as, "A place where we aspire to expand the four limitless qualities of loving-kindness, compassion, joy and equanimity by extending that to others." In doing this prayer, feeling and action are united: we pray for compassion and feed the poor. We heal the part of us that is separate by praying and joining in as part of the solution of problems that all societies create, needs of the peoples and lands and environment.

I want to be part of my time.
When I'm ready,
let prayer lead me to involvement.

Religious historian Diana L. Eck writes about "engaged" Buddhism – the integration of social justice work as Buddhist practice. "Many of America's new Buddhists point to 'engaged Buddhism' as an index of public consequences of personal transformation. Far from being a path toward enlightenment, social Buddhism stems from the seeds of the bodhisattva vow: to save not only oneself, [but] all sentient beings." She details Buddhists involved in hospice care, the growing prison movement, and launching community development ventures such as neighborhood bakeries.

Because I love a schizophrenic brother, all my life I have lived with the feeling "but for the grace of God" goes me. I know my sister feels that, too. He lives in public housing on SSI, a bit of family cash, and the money he makes from playing Scrabble matches. He is a brilliant man now brain damaged by too much thoroxin, he says, a drug that once was given to him to control his paranoid and delusional thinking. Today his speech slurs a bit and he sleeps much of the day and night. He once told me he may be the black sheep of the family but he'll always be mother's little lamb. And, he is right. We all hold him in our memory as the quiet awkward youngster, with big eyes and intellectual curiosity but lacking in the ability to function well in the world. He did nothing to deserve his illness and will never be cured. He doesn't believe in God, but he doesn't not believe either, he tells me, as I tell him of my books.

He does like to sit on the hilly lawn at the side of the projects on late afternoons and feel the breeze. He doesn't pray or ask for much, says he wants his privacy. There is a soulfulness to him as he does, with difficulty, what you and I might do with ease: wash clothes, tend two rooms, make a simple meal. He plays chess and Scrabble and can beat most anyone. People travel to meet with him and try their skill and leave amazed.

Every month he needs extra money which we send. Mother sends "care" packages every month and we help her do so. We have always thought of that as our form of action prayer.

We as a family pray for him. We try to ease his way. The spirit watches him as he lives his life doing the next thing in front of him. The spirit watches our family and asks us to continue to be compassionate especially in times when he withdraws or acts manic. We are entwined and it should be so.

Brothers and sisters, all.

There are many ways to live the life of prayer. I have listened to clients who feel empty who light up when they first volunteer in a grade school classroom teaching creative writing to children who don't have access to tablets and pens and pencils and quiet places at home. To start with ghost stories and lead to what most scares them and express the goblins of their life is the path of healing. To bring a pet to a neighbor and help train that pet, to work at a soup kitchen, to volunteer to have a latchkey child next door come to you for an afternoon snack and talk and quiet time for homework, is to bring the spirit to that table of love. To be willing to get involved with the seeding of the creek or the building of new waterways, all help the world lean toward prayer in action.

> **How can I make a difference?**
> **How can I most be me?**

I know a couple who have adopted several crack cocaine-addicted babies and nursed them to health. Another woman I know volunteers in San Francisco to help runaways living on the streets.

One of the best group efforts I have seen toward living life as a prayer sprang up in San Francisco a few years ago, Care Groups. It started when a woman named Eileen ran an ad in a local paper. She had already brought four women together to meet, bond, and commit to caring for each other in old age, and they were looking for others. The women already committed to the idea were in their early seventies and didn't know each other, although two were already friends. One has a chronic illness with which she is living well and the others have the usual aging stiffness and arthritis but nothing more than that. They interviewed the people who answered and used their intuition to choose four or five who would be a good fit and mix.

All of them are fairly healthy and talked at first about what they each envisioned for the group and each other. They supported each other as they established wills and powers of attorney and proper legal documents. They shared lists of family and friends' names and phone numbers and made agreements about what kind of things they could do to help each other's families and friends when they get sick or needed care.

I asked Eileen what would have happened if someone didn't really respond to the others or like them much. Eileen said that friendship was optional. Loving compassion was essential. Clear enough, I thought, and a larger concept than what I had imagined.

I recently heard that when one member was left without a place to live after her roommate died, the group came to the house and sat in silent prayer with her. Molly was on an oxygen tank and the city had called and said she could have a place in senior housing. The group agreed they would help her move her personal things and let Molly's son know they would pack the lighter stuff. Every day someone came over in the morning and helped her and one day six showed up with food for dinner. She said the silent prayer they did together nourished her but she secretly said her own personal prayer.

> *Thank you for the beauty in this care group.*
> *Thank you for their laughter and warm food.*

She felt her fear of old age and infirmity transformed into a sense of sweet contentment. She knew that when it was her turn she could offer a spare place on her couch or a pot pie or words of encouragement. She had more time than money or energy but she knew she could be there for anyone in her group and wondered why she hadn't done this in early times in her life.

Count on me in sweet contentment.

Practice: Prayer as Action

Sit in prayer aspiring to loving kindness, compassion, joy and equanimity. Perhaps, let it come to the prayer, *As I am* and chant that over and over for ten minutes. Now practice this in your life today with someone who could use a hand and remember prayer as action.

Tipping the balance is all about understanding how important it is to live our lives with others, to pray for our families, our friends, and ourselves in spirit. And to offer what we can.

Human family, blessed be.

As we seek to tip the balance, we pray for the spirit to be a haven for all in our circles and for us to be their port. We develop our own empathy and closeness to others as we come to know our need of them. We try to do some small thing for another each day.

I offer myself in the ways that I can.

In thinking of service as a prayer in action we remember that every major religion asks that we develop qualities that are inherent in spirituality: patience, discipline, effort, meditation or prayer, wisdom, and generosity. In patience, we see ourselves and others as a work in progress and, in discipline, we keep our commitments. We make the effort to be our best selves at all times. Time and experience and our consciousness guide us toward wisdom and, with a generous heart, we both give and receive gifts. We find that service and spiritual practice are truly intertwined!

Rumblings of Change: Activism and Prayer

There is a growing movement afoot to bring progressive political activists to spirituality. One group invites activists to come and walk the ancient labyrinth as a way of connecting with and replenishing spirit. A Jewish leader starts classes to help those activists disfranchised from their culture and religion to find a way to return in a more feminist way. Another activist has started a magazine and calls for spirituality and religion to join to create change.

White Blackwill, a civil rights activist in the 1930s, once said, "We wanted something for ourselves and our children, so we took a chance with our lives." Blackwill used prayer and social justice to change his life and the world. And, it is true, from every slave once held in captivity is the root of any racial freedom we have today.

I'm glad you're free.
I ask to be brought to awareness
so I cause no harm.

In her new book, *War Talk*, Arundahti Roy calls us all to continue bringing the consciousness of corruption of government and corporation to all people in a grassroots way. She feels we must refuse their ideas, their version of history, their wars and weapons, and their notion that nothing can be done.

My prayer,
I am not done in my hope.

Practice: Taking a Stand for Justice and Spirituality
Answer one columnist in your local newspaper on the side of local justice and spirituality.

CHAPTER 20

❦

Praying for Others

Spiritual warrior's pledge:
Not for myself alone, but that all the people may live.
BROOKE MEDICINE EAGLE, *BUFFALO WOMAN COMES SINGING*

In a study done in 1988, Dr Randolph Byrd, a cardiologist at San Francisco General Hospital, tested the usefulness of prayer with all the precautions that we attribute to good science. The results showed that praying for others helped them heal.

Dr Byrd tested prayer in a double-blind clinical situation, with one treatment group being prayed for and one not. He found that regardless of how near or far the pray-er is from the one being prayed for, and regardless of whether the other person *knows* she is being prayed for, praying helps when offered in a compassionate, caring way.

So when you pray for others, pray with compassion and love in your heart. The Buddhists say with "good heart," with no hidden agendas or intent to control another, with no conditions. Just let the spirit work in any way, knowing you are but the instrument of a need to be heard. We don't always know what god's satisfaction will be so if you're unsure of what is best for one you care about, simply ask the best for them or ask them what they might want you to pray.

> *Let the best happen.*
> *Let _____ be helped.*

We pray for others so that the cold wind does not blow on them with too much might or for too long, that they might feel sunshine when it is given. We pray for friends, and the spirit answers because we ask. The spirit likes to help us help our friends. The spirit means to give us power through prayer. It will give to our empty hands because we ask.

> *Help my friends.*
> *Help all people.*

Practice: Praying for the Peoples of the World

The spirit has many voices but the loudest may be yours praying for the peoples of the world. Tonight sit and pray as if you were on a mountain top echoing into the valleys.

Only Prayers That Respect the Other

One of my best friends would find it invasive for someone to pray for her without her permission and knowledge. Her mother, who was abusive to her, openly prays for her daughter's goodness and that she will find her way to God. This is maddening to my friend who remembers the slap of her mother's hand on her face and the feel of the belt buckle on her back. She feels the best "good" she can offer is to have a continuing relationship with her mother where she is kind to her in spite of the beatings. She feels her mother continues to abuse her by believing that she needs religion to make her better.

The misuse of religion has interfered with my friend's ability to find peace with God and I can understand her repulsion. It's not up to me to hurry her path or to decide what is best for her. However, I ask her if I could ask in a compassionate way for the healing of her once-broken ankle that still pains her as she walks; she agrees, as long as I don't use any God talk or the word "prayer."

I promise to call it help from the all-good-in-the-world and she takes my help.

Let her ankle totally heal.

We want to go hiking and camping one last time before summer is over and she'll need to walk a good distance!

Hop, skip, and jump with me in Yosemite woods.

I tell her how I say it and she likes it. She joins me:

Let me hop and skip and jump in Yosemite this summer.

Months later we enjoy the August days and nights near a water-fall with the smell of fir around us, her ankle bound but allowing her to hike without pain. I respected my friend's value system and wishes. Perhaps that's what's healing for her.

We must never pray in a way that attempts to override or disrespects someone else's values. They get to decide what help to take from us. We must pray wanting only for their good.

You might think of this as you would trying to give a friend a gift because *you* like it. Perhaps some perfume. It's just the light fragrance you like. However, your friend doesn't believe in wearing scents and is conscious of others with allergies. She would prefer unscented lotions and creams. Would you give your friend what you want or follow her beliefs? Give prayers of the heart in a way with which you can both live comfortably.

I care.
I want the best for you.
You are in my heart.
I wish you well.
I care for you.

Practice: Praying for Someone Else

Ask one friend if there is a prayer you could say for them and if so, what it would be. Pray that prayer for them.

Charlie Thom, a Karuk native American medicine man, explains his prayer role in Bobby Lake-Thom's book *Spirits of the Earth*. A medicine man must go to the mountain or some other power center to pray for his people. That is his job. Charlie Thom says, "I connect with the power and shoot it straight down from the mountaintop into the sacred dance. It is like a beam of light, or electricity. It will make the healing more powerful. It strengthens the dancers. And I ask the spirits from the mountain to come down and dance with us in the ceremony, as our ancestors originally did in the Beginning."

Reading these lines, a client of mine went up Mount Tam shortly before her cousin's death and prayed down on the rooftops of the town, the rooftop of the home of her cousin and asked that her cousin be released from suffering. She said it felt good to pray for her cousin from a different perspective and wished she had thought of going on a vision quest to take the vision of her cousin to a healing place but her death came too soon.

She said it occurred to her in praying those last six months of her young cousin's life that she was ready to be part of the answer and that she had asked god to find the strength to help in any way necessary. She had found herself close at hand, at bedside, and felt this was her way to be part of the solution of less suffering. She felt that she and her cousin were prayer partners both holding up the vision of a belief in the spirit of life and the journey toward mysteries.

Practice: Finding a Power Place

Find a power place from which to send your prayers. Let it be an exploration over a period of time and enjoy the search.

※

CHAPTER 21

Praying with Others

Prayer is the natural language of love.
JOAN BROWN CAMPBELL, IN JIM CASTELLI'S *HOW I PRAY*

We know that people have been praying pretty much since the beginning of time. In early centuries, prayers were shared around stone circles and fires, in chant and dance for the well-being of the community; tree leaves stood for letters of the alphabet and were used in the passing of messages; and spirit energy lived in the earth and its people.

Recently, I was part of a circle with Christina Baldwin, author of *The Seven Whispers,* and was reminded how good it felt to be part of a circle with the energy holding the eighteen of us, behind the back of the chairs and below us like a bowl. It was all encompassing. We talked and wrote about spirituality in our lives and, with drumming, allowed our bodies to feel whispers of peace of mind and accepting the pace of guidance. I had forgotten what a strong connection a circle makes between people when the intent is honest sharing with each other.

I have always thought of intuitive whispers as prayers that come to us when we are most relaxed: gardening, walking,

praying. The sharing of whispers with a group makes the practice of listening to intuition or prayer even more real. It is the
witnessing of our belief in others and the experiencing of the
heightened group energy that makes prayer become more alive.

Hearts beating together,
spirits alive.

One of the best reasons to pray with a group is that it helps us
learn to be one. As we fold our hands together, or upward, or
join hands loosely in a circle, we feel the loving intent of other
humans in the group. We hear their prayers with our hearts
and bodies, understand their callings. Honesty and earnestness
breaks feelings of separation and we know we are not alone and
unable to cope but rather we are undergirded by concern. In
just hearing another's prayers, we will change.

I feel the rumbles in the weather of my being.

Practice: A Part of the Human Race

In prayer, see yourself alone on a rock near a gentle
stream. Now see yourself with another. Then a small
group. Then a large group. Feel the energy build and
change as you sit dreaming together gazing at the river.
Relax into being a part of the human race. Write a prayer.

I define community as a place where you can speak your heart and
know that you will be respected for that effort. Others may agree or

not, but community allows for you to be yourself among them. You are granted acceptance and offer acceptance and in that principle on which the group is built all are safe from criticism or rejection.

Practice: Starting a Prayer Community

You can start a prayer community with just a few friends or like-minded spiritual people. I suggest that you meet and clarify what each of you is seeking. Perhaps it is an open forum for discussion and prayer of the mysteries of the spirit. Perhaps religion and faith are not an issue but rather a shared desire to be open to living day-to-day and accepting spirit in life as it unfolds. This core group forms a vision for the group and then asks others to join the circle if they share in that vision.

Then just meet and try out different ways of running your group. Most groups gather in a circle, all members facing each other, signifying that all are equal. As each participant faces the center, the energy of the group is pulled to the center of the circle. You are encompassed by the circle as the world outside recedes and this sacred place becomes your focus. Here you are in connection with others and spirit.

You might want to select a leader or have rotating leadership or no leadership at all. You might choose to read something (either explicitly spiritual or not) together before each meeting and then open the meeting by sharing thoughts of how you were affected by what you read.

The leader, if you have one, might then offer some prayers for the day. Or you might want to see what's on the minds of the people attending and create your prayers around the needs of the moment.

One good device I've used to ensure that no one interrupts is a walking stick. Any stick, simple to elaborate, can be used. Whoever is speaking holds the stick. When they are through, they pass it. But while the stick is being held, no interruptions are permitted.

Be sure to leave time for feedback on how/if the circle is meeting the needs of the members.

Your prayer group has begun.

Prayer community can be especially helpful when we are tired of life and tired of prayer; this is when we need to depend on others to keep us going. You can go to your group to be held in prayer as you are held up united in spiritual belief. When you are weak, your community can hold you strong. When you are ready to rise again, you'll walk the prayer path feeling even more connected to those spirits on earth that cared enough to be with you through weariness and doubt.

Practice: Finding a Prayer Partner

Some of us work best with a prayer partner – a friend or acquaintance who we talk to about our prayers. I found that my daughter-in-law is easy to talk to about prayer and we share ideas of new visions and hold each other dear. You may already be doing this with someone in your life or you may need to seek out those who might feel safe and talk about prayer or actually pray together silently or in ritual.

CHAPTER 22

Praying for Love of Country and the World

Prayer is the law of the universe.
You don't even have to believe in God to Ask.

Sophy Burnham, *A Book of Angels*

Early on the morning of September 11, 2001, my son called to see if I had heard the news about the terrorist attack on the World Trade Center in New York and to find out if I was okay. I hadn't heard anything because I was starting my writing day at home in the quiet manner with which I begin most days: prayer, a walk by the water, eating a light breakfast, writing out a work schedule for the day. I turned on the television as he talked to me and watched the second tower crumble before my eyes.

He told me all that he knew and I found myself reassuring him and promising to call that evening. I sat for a moment and discovered my hands folded in prayer, a gesture that sprang from childhood days in the white-washed church with the single cross. I thought of my family. The immediate response of prayer and family seemed a comfort to me. I was in a kind of disassociated shock and I found myself simply saying, *Help them, help the families,* as I imagined the killings and the suffering, the loss of life.

Blessed be the victim, the dead and injured. Help us all.

I was aware of my connection to the lives of those workers who were mothers and fathers, spouses, significant others, and family members just like the loved ones in my life.

We are one. Human.

My mind seemed to ramble through associations of my experiences and how a life can change in a moment and how life is both precious and delicate. Nancy Griffith's song. Lost in my own associations and thoughts, needing time, I wanted quiet. I turned off the television knowing I would hear the story of who and what and why when I was ready.

During the moments of silence I had given myself I wondered: "What do I do with this silent time?" There was no question that I would pray. Prayer seemed to be a natural response. But for what? I found myself not wanting to pray a petition asking for mercy. The deed had been done. I don't believe men are evil although I know firsthand that there is evil in the world and that men do evil deeds.

I walked over to my favorite window, what I call my "writing window" and could smell the sweet lilac pressed against the glass and noticed how lilacs shelter me from my neighbors' view and too much light. I stood there looking at this bit of nature wondering about life and human nature. I wanted to be part of the solution to an uncertain world.

I wanted the world to be kind. Most of all, I wanted this not to have happened.

Let me be part of the solution.

I prayed for stability in the world. I prayed for a measured response from our government, and gentleness for the wounded and survivors who had lost loved ones. I prayed for those killed and those who were frightened in their last moments. I thanked my spirit for all good in the world, those who would help, those who transform because of this seemingly meaningless tragedy. I remembered a part of a prayer from the Bible:

Yea, though I walk through the valley of death,
thy rod will comfort me.

I was comforted by the beauty of the words of the Bible. They were the words from Sunday school days of my childhood. I prayed that men wouldn't try to solve this tragedy with the same mindset that had caused it. In the 2500 years since women lost a voice in the Church, cultures harbor men as both leaders and followers that will use misguided violence in the service of right and only God. Personalities created from the seed of twisted hatred, from lives of abuses and neglects, will go too far. I thought of a quote from Booker T. Washington: "More and more we must learn to think not in terms of race or color or language or religion or of political boundaries, but in terms of humanity. Above all races and political boundaries there is humanity."

In the face of such devastating tragedy, we can pray:

May strength and wisdom enter our healing.
May cooperation reign.
May the hurt be held in the arms of care.
May goodness rise from the ash.

I listened to the echoes of the past and the stretch of 35,000 years and knew those years would have much to say if we could but listen. I wondered what it would be like to stop competing and start cooperating.

Let there be a new beginning.

I watched my mind wandering, trying to sort out feelings of grief and anger. I was glad to be writing a book on prayer to connect us to the spirit. Prayers to hold as a vehicle for change.

Let us be all things.

I was glad to have prayer alive in my life and to feel that prayer could comfort me. Prayers made a difference! I wanted at that moment to "fix" things, but also knew that I could not but could be part of the solution. I could help tip the balance.

I offered my energy. I could pray for help for our nation.

Let us be united in grief.
Guide us.
Reflective consideration.
Temperate action.
Spirit, be with us.

Before we rush to fix things we must also ask ourselves three questions:

- "Did they ask for help?"
- "Would it empower them if I helped?"
- "Do I have it to give right now?"

If the answer to any of those questions is "No," we must not offer to "fix" or help or at least give ourselves time to think things through.

Practice: Before We Rush to Fix

Think of a situation large or small important in your life and answer the three questions above. How does it make you feel? Is there any change to how you would normally help? Make a prayer out of any realization you have.

When I felt ready, I turned on the television again and watched as a group of New Yorkers observed a few moments of silence. I joined them in spirit. Later, my partner Pat and I went to the Metropolitan Community Church in San Francisco to hear Reverend Penny Nixon talk of grief and healing. We prayed for the victims of the terrorists and their spirits. We prayed for their lives and their death. We asked to be part of all people who would pray for the best: healing after grief and forgiveness in the face of disaster.

Healing after grief, forgiveness after disaster.

I prayed again with love for those who were denied a full life to develop their potential or feel their joy. I prayed that those left behind would remember in time that even after loss there is always something left to love. I prayed to be authentic, not merely good, to help the world deal with their shadow selves, their angers and resentments.

I felt that the real war was the conflict within humans that allows evil behavior to result from our hatred. As the breeze moves through the valley in the late afternoon, love or hate touches all humans. I prayed:

As we touch life, may our actions be guided.

My prayers seemed to be saying, by praying and acting well, together we could bring about a period of spiritual peace and understanding. Also, and most importantly:

I am sorry. I am sorry for you and your loved ones.

Several weeks later I listened to a show on public radio where they were discussing Margaret Mead's findings as a social anthropologist in the 1930s on the South Pacific island of New Guinea. Someone mentioned that Mead's ideas about creating systems that are healthy for all and all inclusive were becoming important again as we search for constructive ways to be in the world as a nation. This after her research had been discredited through the years because Western "civilization" was unable to accept *diversity* and other as our own. In *New Lives for Old*, Mead writes:

"When the pattern is too narrow in relationship to the possibilities of human variation and existing patterns in the outside world, then the system can only maintain itself by extruding or excluding those who rebel against narrowness, and those who rebel against the narrowness, and those who remain become narrower still. Movements with potentiality for change are able to modify the new system to allow for change."

Practice: Rebelling Against Narrowness
Talk Mead's idea over with a thoughtful friend.

And so we must be careful with groups, whether governments or cults, when we see the narrowness of leaders who allow no new ideas or criticisms.

We watch as governments rush to judgment of who is right and who is wrong. Although we morally know the difference between right and wrong, if we are committed to tipping the balance we hesitate to blame without looking at the context of the violence or wrongdoing. Even in the United States, only one representative, Barbara Lee, felt safe enough to vote against the rush to war against Afghanistan, the other members of the House and Senate afraid of being ostracized and seen as non-patriotic. As time goes by, reasoned and spiritual people are starting to show their disagreement with military might against a small, weak country.

Other ways. Possibilities of peace that last.

Those of us committed to tipping the balance look carefully for an attitude of openness where the goal is harmony and alignment. We recognize that the only real liberation comes about when we liberate the oppressed *and* the oppressor from pain and suffering. As we seek harmony and alignment, we strive to find the heart to pity and forgive those who act against them.

Our prayers of the heart are guided from within.

Allow our hearts to open to listen.
Let us understand all sides.

We now know that 9/11 was just a beginning of a new age of war and terrorism and we recognize the urgency of making a difference in our personal life, community life, and country's life, and globally. What we must do is bring the soft heart of activism to affect change and know that freedom includes duty:

I let my voice be heard.
Peace in me. Peace in you. Peace all around us. Peace for all
of us. We are enveloped in peace.
No war for profit. Peace for all.
I am a part of my times. I help create a peaceful family.
I help create a peaceful workplace. I help create a peaceful
community. I help create a peaceful world.

Sometimes the problems of the world would have us duck our heads, turn off the news, and get away from troubles we can't do anything about and that come from a kind of competitive thinking we are working to change in ourselves and all of us. I like the ideas of Margaret Silf in her book *Close to the Heart* as she talks about the shrinking world method, "So … a way of praying the heart especially when the news is too much for you, might be to seek out a real person amid the carnage and let that one person's story, that one person's heart, form your prayer of intercession. This will shrink the unmanageable down to a size that is unavoidable."

What might it look like to love your enemies? Questions such as this feel dangerously tangible to me. Recently, Betsy Rose, who organizes songs at peace marches, asked others to sing "How could anyone ever tell you you were anything less than beautiful?" to whatever enemy we saw in our mind's eye. This is the practice of prayer.

I hold good in my heart for the people of our country and the world.

We pray because we desire a peaceful and spiritual society. We pray for those in leadership that they might be wise and consider the problems that plague our country from a spiritual perspective. We pray for the people influencing others such as ministers, teachers, social workers, mothers, and nurses.

We ask that they consider the spirit of those they encounter and use their training to help encourage the lost and those in their care. We ask that workers be blessed with far-seeing so that they might look at their lives as worthy in the eyes of god and the spirit of the machinery of the world; we ask that they bring peace and calm to their job environments and homes.

Let's pray for a nation where we use our wealth and size to lead others to cooperative help for all peoples and lands. Let's be the nation who spreads seeds of generosity in compassionate help. Let's use our leadership to lead the way to a humane world, where men and women can live equally and freely, believing in a spirit of choice.

Let's long for a better world with ourselves as one of the centers of positive change. It is with this awareness that we stand with our hands outstretched, open to the spirit. We feel ourselves as the vastness of the human heart connected to the world.

See us now, open to the vastness of life.

In prayer we change ourselves and we change the world. As we become the holder of grace, we give an ease to the troubled world. We are the ripple in the water that gently reaches the bank, quivers down to the depth of the river and touches the bedrock bottom, affects the flow of the river to the mouth of the ocean. Even when we don't see this effect, it is happening; change grows not out of our ripple but within it.

Prayer helps see beyond hurt and anger and reminds us that we are united with the world. We learn through prayer not to make other people and lands dangerous. We heal the hurt and fear that creates patterns of avoidance toward certain peoples and lands that we falsely judge. We ask the imagination to heal us all and the world.

Recently I stood with a group called Hands Around the Lake on the anniversary of the assassination of Martin Luther King, Jr. We held hands and formed a chain all the way around Lake Merritt in Oakland, California, to honor the lives of King and Mahatma Gandhi. The objective was to provide a powerful experience of community, of a community that shares the vision of a world free of violence, hate, and intolerance. Move On, the group that organized the event, prefers to affirm *for* peace rather than protest *against* war. Gandhi and King strongly believed in the power of affirmation. In this light, we came together to express our common humanity and to affirm for peace in the world at large and here in Oakland as well.

I long for a community of kind hearts to walk the days with me, reminding and nurturing the best in me.
Let the group start with me.

We need our prayers to ask for a foreign policy based on survival of humanity rather than national interests. Can you imagine celebrating common humanity? What if we prayed for a shared life among the peoples of the world?

We need to pray for new leaders; men and women who will speak out openly and with conviction that peace is stronger than any war.

Let's pray for peace on earth. Let's pray for our heart's desires that puts good into the world.

All people, all things living for good.

CHAPTER 23

⚘

Prayers for the Earth that is a Part of Us

How shall I celebrate the planet
that, even now, carries me
in its fruited womb?

DIANE ACKERMAN, THE PLANETS

Of course we are not just peoples of nations but creatures of this earth, and so we can use our prayers to affirm our connection and our interconnected responsibility to our earth.

> **Let me step into the circle.**
> **Let me step into the circle of life.**

Prayer can be a posture toward life that says we are interconnected. It says people are interrelated; we need help and offer thanks to the spirit. It is lining ourselves up with all living things.

> **This is what I want to happen, that our earth mother**
> **be clothed in ground snow**
> **in rest before the time of seed and planting,**
> **then the season of blossom and fruit.**

That fire clear the forest but just enough,
the birds gathering thistle, willow, and cottonwood,
the mountain shielding the valley from winds and too
much rain,
the spruce growing in the shade of aspen,
fir in the shade of yellow pine.
Into the bodies of stars and the round bright sun
life beamed, given and returned to the sky,
I give this prayer, my drum alive.

As we step into the knowledge that we are the world, the rain, the berry on the winter bush, the bloom in summer, we find that our prayers change to include ourselves and all others. And we pray:

I am the world, myself, all living beings.

We pray for the good earth and give thanksgiving as the Zunis do:

We are grateful,
O Mother Earth
For the mountains
and the streams
Where the deer, by command of your
Breath of life, shall wander.
Wishing for you the
fullness of life.
We shall go forth prayerfully upon
the trails of our Earth Mother.

Practice: Becoming a Cloud Watcher

Become a cloud watcher and notice the puddles after the rain.

Water, oceans of my life.

Practice: Pray to the Trees

Hike in the woods and pray to the trees:

I remember you.

If the trees answer, be grateful.

Practice: Praying for Your Earth's Body

See how much fun it can be to develop a spiritual and imaginative connection with a friend or even a new person. Ask that new friend who will play with you in the world of the unseen to pray for your earth's body.

Together we belong.

Pray to put visions of transformation into the world, to give us forests of green, fresh sparkling water, fish that leap the waterfalls into our arms.

All of us, forest and fish, human, together – treasures.

Yes, let us not forget the other creatures with whom we share the planet. Jane Goodall, the social anthropologist, has brought us stories from Tanzania and helped us understand the value of chimpanzees as soulful sentient creatures who can form attachments and offer love, nurturing, and kindness.

In her book *Reason for Hope: A Spiritual Journey*, she explores her personal spiritual odyssey and asks us to open ourselves to "the saints" within each of us. Goodall feels there are four reasons to continue to have faith in millennia ahead:

1   The human brain;
2   The resilience of nature;
3   The energy and enthusiasm that is found or can be kindled among young people worldwide; and
4   The indomitable human spirit.

I am sure each of us has personal stories that would substantiate these reasons for hope. The human mind that is capable of inventing electricity, telescopes, and ice cream served on sugar cones can surely be used for the good of peace for sentient beings: the ferns that grow in the marshes, the trees with their leafy wings, and animals alive with spirit deserving a place among us.

Let us pray for protection and care of all dependent creatures and safe-keeping of the animals in the wild. Let us ask that animals hunted for meat be treated without torture and animals trapped for eating be treated humanely. Let us remember through prayer that animals are a part of us and perhaps decide to forgo meat and chicken and fish more often than usual, or completely. At the very least, let us give thanks for the gift of their bodies and ask for our body to be held in spirit. Let us remember that whether it is the warming day or the licorice night, a spirit tugs at us and asks us to be conscious and humane.

Let's learn to follow the patience of the slow-growing lichen, the knowledge of swift rivers in the waters of the fish, and from the roar of the lion and elephant. Let's live like the California poppy at the side of the road: taking sun and water as offered and giving brilliant beauty each year as spring turns to summer.

Let us remember that the rocks and stones of our world are alive in spirit and give thanks for the stones at the river's bottom, clear water. Let us remember that we are interconnected with their history of life.

I wrote this poem after returning home from a walk to the far end of a beach in Santa Cruz, where the stones were piled high and provided places to rest and watch the dawn. Again, the sweet gum tree.

At the window of my sweet gum tree,
I teach stones to talk,
croon them soft with consonants,
coax the vowels out of marble,
beseech the ghost in the core of granite
to loosen its grip on the grate
that separates us –
beg slabs of rock to toss
their fossiled footprints and
gamboled tracings across the page.

Recently, I spoke to a group of eighteen-year-olds who had come to San Francisco from Sacramento, California, to participate in the peace marches protesting the war in Iraq. They were fresh from the large Saturday march and felt high-spirited, talking of taking the path to cooperation in this world. They did not seem to resent the police for arresting them and didn't have negative things to say about the way the large crowds were handled.

I remembered back to the trespasses of the Chicago police in 1968 during the Vietnam War and thought of how far we had come in awareness and training. These kids in San Francisco knew that the police, as authority, were not the problem. The problem was war for money and they knew that and respected the police who were doing their high-stress job with restraint and compassion.

The youngsters focus on the peace in themselves and we chant together:

Let peace begin with me.
Let me be an instrument.
Let me be the voice of peace.
Let peace begin with me.

The indomitable human spirit Goodall speaks of is around us in the every day: just think of all the people with special needs who use public transportation to get to work and live as normal a life as they can; the children from incredibly abusive backgrounds who find role models and dream and succeed; artists brave enough to hold on to their vision of the need for imagination in the world and find ways to live a lifetime on the edge of financial insecurity.

We have all seen war – and the destruction it brings for centuries to come – win over peace, dishonesty compete with honesty, and manipulation accepted as part of the business game. Even with all that, those of us committed to tipping the balance back toward love and compassion are growing in numbers as the years go by.

> *More than kindness know, let me in kindness act.*
> *Let me find my way to children's door*
> *so that I may find in the full smile of their face*
> *a healing force.*
> *Let me find a child*
> *who needs a sewn bear and warm milk.*
> *The human spirit longs for peace among the flocks*
> *and together we share our cupped hands.*

Prayer can change our lives and lead us to new beliefs and actions of harmony. Prayer practice can be one action that helps us tread lightly on our mother ground.

I live on this earth with grace and caring.

"Spirituality is the sacred center," writes Christina Baldwin, in *Life's Companion*, "out of which all life comes, including Mondays and Tuesdays and rain Saturday afternoons in all their mundane and glorious detail … The spiritual journey is the soul's life co-mingling with ordinary life."

As sentient beings we know our breath is held in the mystery of life and its forecasted death.

Something has been lost in the world but I believe it can be

found. I think the true discovery of living is but a few generations away and I am ready to be part of the solution by giving
up the small picture and being re-born into a larger one.

If you are not sure, then take just a step toward personal
prayer and you may realize that when you were not on a spiritual path you could only see your own point of view or the
view of today. By opening your heart to prayer, we lose our
point of view and shift to a moving, changing truth that is
unfettered by fear.

Just to start begins it all.

Practice: Honoring Your Changing Truth

Tell a friend your changing truth about how you are
living. Ask your friend to share her truth and ask her to
ask another and so on, creating a chain of people
pondering this.

Spirituality is rooted in longing and until the day we cease
longing, we can create something new in ourselves and the
world. As sentient beings we desire something we can never see
or name, but which nevertheless embraces us in the days and
nights of breath and lives just beyond our fingertips. It is in this
mystery that we all become one in prayer.

Our prayer: always
the human race, our family circle,
the bird and the bear,
hollyhocks and forget-me-nots –
one embrace –
the mud body of earth.

∗

Recommended Reading

Prayer/Spiritual/Affirming Books

Benson, Robert, *Living Prayer*, Jeremy P. Tarcher/Putnam, New York, NY, 1998

Chodron, Pema, *The Wisdom of No Escape*, Shambhala Publications, Boston, MA, 1991

Ciaravino, Helene, *How to Pray*, Square One Publishers, Garden City Park, NY, 2001

Dossey, Larry, M.D., *Prayer is Good Medicine*, HarperSanFrancisco, San Francisco, CA, 1996

Gawain, Shakti, *The Path of Transformation*, New World Library, Novato, CA, 2000

Hagen, Steve, *Buddhism Plain and Simple*, Tuttle Publishing, Boston, MA, 1997

Hanh, Thich Nhat, *The Blooming of a Lotus*, Beacon Press, Boston, MA, 1993

Klausner, Henriette Anne, *Write It Down, Make It Happen*, Scribner, New York, NY, 2000

Matthews, Caitlin, *The Celtic Book of Days*, Destiny Books, Rochester, Vermont, 1995

Padilla, Stan, *Chants and Prayers*, Book Publishing Company, Summertown, TN, 1995

Palmer, Parker, *The Active Life*, HarperCollins, New York, NY, 1990

Rainier, Tristine, *The New Diary*, Jeremy P. Tarcher, New York, NY, 1978

Roberts, Elizabeth, Amidon, Elias, *Earth Prayers*, HarperSanFrancisco, San Francisco, CA, 1991

Sheehy, Gail, *Passages*, Bantam Books, New York, New York, 1976

Silf, Margaret, *Close to the Heart: A Guide to Personal Prayer*, Loyola Press, Chicago, IL, 1999

Starhawk, *The Spiral Dance*, Harper and Row, San Francisco, CA, 1979

Sweeney, Jon M., *Praying with Our Hands*, Skylight Paths Publishing, Woodstock, VT, 2000

Thom, Bobby-Lake, *Spirits of the Earth*, Plume Books, New York, 1997

Walsh, Roger, *Essential Spirituality*, John Wiley & Sons, New York, 1999

Zander, Rosamund Stone and Zander, Benjamin, *The Art of Possibility*, Harvard Business School Press, Boston, MA, 2000

Poetry Volumes

Dillard, Annie, *Mornings Like This*, Harper Perennial, New York, NY, 1995

Merwin, W.S., *The Rain in the Trees*, Alfred A. Knopf, New York, NY, 1993

Neruda, Pablo, *Stones of the Sky*, Copper Canyon Press, Port Townsend, WA, 1970

Oliver, Mary, *New and Selected Poems*, Beacon Press, Boston, MA, 1992

Ondaatje, Michael, *The Cinnamon Peeler*, Vintage International, New York, NY, 1989

Valentine, Jean, *Pilgrims*, Carnegie Mellon University Press, Pittsburgh, PA, 1995

Quotation Books

Cook, John, *The Book of Positive Quotations*, Fairview Press, Minneapolis, MN, 1997

Newman, Richard, *African American Quotations*, Checkmark Books, New York, New York, 2003

Partnow, Elaine, *The Quotable Woman*, Facts on File, Inc. New York, NY, 1977

Safransky, Sy, *Sunbeams: A Book of Quotations*, The Sun Publishing Company, 1990

Warner, Carolyn, *Treasury of Women's Quotations*, Prentice-Hall, Inc., Englewood Cliffs, NJ, 1992

꙳

The Prayers

Introduction

- Blessed be. A place for me.
- Let me embrace what I believe with others at my side. All of it.
- Each, belongs. A new welcoming.
- God, Buddha, Allah, Goddess, Father/Mother Spirit, lead me to gardens holding pools of water.
- Old Wise One, lead me to gardens holding pools of water.
- Let this tiny house hold the sadness of the world. Help me find connection and peace.
- I am included in all things. Thank you, dear spirit, for holding hope while I learn to trust my heart.
- I give praise for the little feet of love around the world. Lift me to the light in the trees. Let me begin with acceptance and end with transformation. Footprints and sand, together, earthbound prayer.
- Hold me.
- Guide me.
- Raindrop, all I need.
- I'm blessed with nights of lightning bugs flickering their wand before me, finches bringing messages from departed ones, days when grass glows neon, and the heavens, mirrors of fish and flora in glass lakes.

- Help me see beyond what I can see. Let me enjoy this clay land and quiet. Spirit, maker, mother, father, me. Thank you for ripe summer.
- Heart, spirit, let me be with you.
- Yes.
- Beauty, everywhere.
- Love.
- Thank you.
- I am wanted in prayer.
- Spirit, in me shine.
- May the best be done.
- May we find deep meaning in life that lives at our fingertips. Just look at our hands, they are ablaze!

Part One: Prayers of Wonder

- Thank you for the quiet of the day. I am not alone. All of us, new song of earth.

Chapter 1: Saying Thank You
- Thank you for my life. Thank you for all, here with me. Thank you for my part in the whole.
- I have been given much.
- Life, and all its tiny moments. Thank you.
- There is everything here for me.
- Haven of my day.
- Wonder, I notice and create.
- Thank you for life.
- I'm alive with spirit.

- Thank you, spirit, for my friend. Thank you for helping me feel love that's offered.
- Beauty all around. Season, each lovely. My heart, people in my life. Thanks and praise, life as it is.
- Many helped in ways I needed but could not see. Thank you.
- Thank you for the new growth outside my window.
- Thank you for high boots and warm feet.
- Why am I here? What is my ground? Where is my spirit body? Why must I pray? What are some things that stay? Do I listen to the song or the singer? Why are we gathered here? What is my heartbeat? What can silence give me? Why is nothing a good thing? Where is death? Why should I wish for a string of pearls? Why does the abyss gaze at me? How can I repack my old trunk? What is it I don't know I love so much? What way do I find shelter? How can I reach the place I can't find? How can I help the core of the apple earth?

Chapter 2: Praying to the Part of Us That is Spirit

- We do not live chartless; we live in the wave of the spirit.
- I pray to my spirit; kind, loving all life.
- The spirit flows through me and is me.
- All things, me. Light and goodness, be.
- Hills and valleys, let me touch the ground.
- Every step I take is on the path of prayer.

Chapter 3: Praying in Focused Attention

- As a bud is to a blossom, prayer is to the spirit.
- I am spirit.
- I am the light, I am the light. I belong to the world in love.
- Prayers of wonder, everywhere.

- As far as the eye can see, the creation of sand and its forms meeting the ebb and flowing sea. I belong here. I am part of this.

Chapter 4: Coming Into the Present

- I am alive with feeling. I bless my body.
- As I feel my body, I feel my spirit.
- Here it is. Life and spirit, our daily bread.
- Thank you for this day, the loving people in my life, the bird outside my window.
- As I touch, let me be touched.
- Praise to the child that may someday come through me. Praise to my husband and all things gentle
- I am a person of worth. I find the balance. I see the glory in the world as it is and I am part of that glory.
- I am all things. I pray for all things. One spirit, one life, goodness abounds.
- I did my best and sometimes it wasn't good enough. I'm sorry. I offer possibilities. I offer praise for possibilities of healing our sorrows, and living our lives.
- As it is, I am content. As it could be, I vision and work.
- I praise the hand that holds me.

Chapter 5: Offering Ourselves to Prayer

- My life of hardship and taffy, I offer.
- Here I am. Hands up. Lead me.
- Thank you for long nights of sleep and healthy eating, a walk and a swim.
- Thank you for the change I needed.
- Thank you. The world is good. People are good. Good things happen to me. I give and receive help.

- I am puzzled by, but praise, the letting go.
- We humans, find peace within, and grow a world of peace without.
- Thank you for helping me find my prayer. Thank you for the imagination and searching of my son.
- Thank you for friendship: seed, blossom, and berry.
- A journey, each of us, a way.
- I feel the good of all sentient beings.
- Thank you for the song in my heart.

Part Two: Prayers of Possibility

- Let me wander in holy groves among sacred trees – peace in the heart of the day.
- Quiet, let me find myself.

Chapter 6: Asking for Help

- Steady path, steady footstep.
- Loved in my need, blessed be.
- Sitting in the heart of spirit.
- Lend me a bough for help.
- I ask for help developing patience and trusting that in time I will see what's right for me. I know when to hold on; I know when to let go. Please help me trust that you are with me, spirit.
- Guide my path.
- Time and prayer on my side. Spirit, guide me to what I need to learn.
- We are our fear and more than our fear. We give our thanks and gifts to the world.

- My mind filled with love for flecks of dust a tiny shell, grey feathers, the wind, the ocean, the bird in flight.
- May the blessing of light be on you – light without and light within. May the blessed sunlight shine on you and warm your heart until it glows like a great peat fire.
- May your day be touched by a bit of Irish luck, brightened by a song in your heart, and warmed by the smiles of the people you love.
- I hear you at the corner store, see you in the glow of light in a painting of the forest, touch you on my child's shoulder. Everywhere, spirit. I long for your presence. It is given.
- Help me.
- Guided to your care. It is given.
- Let time be my friend. Help us heal.
- Layers of myself, revealed.
- Blessed be, you and me.
- Let me be a vehicle for positive change.
- Good heart, carry on.
- Spirit, let me find you.
- When I hold more than my body can bear, I let go into the sea and become a bottle thrown, new wishes and hopes a'floating.

Chapter 7: Prayer Methods, Direct vs. Indirect

- I am my best self in prayer.
- I am clear. I don't want to argue anymore. Bring peace to my life. Let me learn to talk differently, allowing others to disagree while I remain calm.
- Spirit, give _____ what she needs to heal. Spirit, pay attention to _____.
- Let _____ earn more money. Let _____ prosper.

- Help me earn more money. Help me feel secure.
- Let me travel to Greece. Fuel my imagination.
- Heal my sore joints. Heal my body.
- Watch over _____'s safe return. Keep _____ safe.
- The spirit knows. Thy will be done.
- God, Goddess, Spirit, guide me to your side.
- Thy will be done.
- Spirit of all, Spirit of all.
- We all deserve happiness and harmony. So be it.

Chapter 8: Prayers for Clarifying Our Beliefs and Goals

- Let my path be known to me. Let me see the way. Under my pen, my feelings known. Let feelings lead the way to truth. I ask that I trust how I feel. I ask to know the best for all. I listen. I question. I believe. I listen. I question. I believe.
- In this circle, we place ourselves as boughs blowing in the wind and plants that seed the earth. We call the fire of the sun to fuel our lives and waters to sweep over our wrongdoings. We ask stone to hold good firm in our hearts, and, in the hard land of earth, find a cold surface of slate to cool the heat of May. Fed from plains of crown corn growing, we pray: Oh God, oh Goddess, blessed be.
- Always I am beginning anew again.
- As I create, I am in spirit.
- Blooming now.
- I am cocooned with my spirit. I know who I am.
- Here I am, a wreck. Be with me.
- Here I am taking care.
- Thank you for noticing my light.
- Thank you for your light. Thank you for listening.

- Help me care and yet be separate.
- Give me friends I can trust.

Chapter 9: Prayers for Emotional Healing

- Just me, sitting in the boil of anger looking for spirit. Let spirit find me. Here!
- Prayer practice, that's what this is. I bring a longing to prayer.
- Even this feeling in me I can love.
- I am a good person and have all my feelings including anger. It's safe to be mad. I leak anger out as it comes up. I turn my attention to myself sometimes. I express my feelings with love. I express anger. Day to day. Little ways. People love me even though I tell my truth. In every way every day I am getting more authentic. I don't hurt myself or others with my anger. I learn to be compassionate with my anger.
- I am a good person even if I have anger. I can express my anger in the every day in a kind way.
- Spirit, I accept your guidance.
- Keep me safe.
- I am responsible to feel and express. I do so without injuring others.
- Tell stories and I come. Tell stories and I come. I sit under the sun and the sun shines bright. I pull on the cloud and the cloud gives rain. With plenty of food from the earth, I sing. I sing again with a belly full of corn. I am the sun and the cloud and the rain. I am the food and the earth. I am the corn.
- I forgive myself. I forgive you. I understand shortcomings. I understand misunderstandings. I understand myself in human nature.
- You are the best part of me.

- As I am, not perfect. As I try to be, better.
- Let each be seen for their good contribution. May I be seen and valued. May I see and value my work. Spirit, may I connect with you.
- We are all the same and different. I choose to be here with my family.
- Always with spirit or about to be.
- When I can no longer stand the flesh of my anger reddened and seething holding on to grievances and every wrongdoing, and I am most in hatred, I ask rescue.
- This is my prayer: a journey where life flows through me, felt and accepted, moving like the turning seasons, the storm that harms or nourishes but passes. This is my prayer: grace with forgiveness, an arrow shot through the storm to sun and light.
- Let me accept my journey.
- Release me from hurt. Release me from feelings of revenge. Release anger from my body. Let me give this to you, spirit, so I can be free.
- Let my prayers take me deep into myself so that I might find I possess exactly what I desire.
- Help me live through this.
- I am asked to accept the unacceptable and I don't know how. Help me.
- As I live, I find a way.
- I do not have to understand. Guide me, spirit. Hold me, rock me.
- All things in life, death, return, my life.
- Blessed be, _____ in the trees and hillsides. Let me know you are with me as I am with you.
- Lonely. I am lonely, I wail. I wait.
- As I pray, I become.
- You are remembered with love and respect. You are part of the

common thread that binds us together. You are part of the tribe.
We, together.

- Young and old, life continuing.
- Blessed are the dead, souls in peace.
- Feed our mouths just as you feed our spirits, this oh Loas, we beg.
- Spirit, the many drums you hear are our wishes to find you.
- I held on to all my losses like stones in my pockets until, one day at the bank of the river, I saw moss and mud clinging to stone and realized stones belonged to the world and not me.
- Emptying my pockets at the river's edge, my heart lightened. I felt a freedom. With the damp body of nature turned toward me, I felt a breeze of promise returning.
- I long for promise returning. Let me feel the breeze.
- The spirit holds me as I walk the earth.
- The circle is open, but unbroken. May the peace of the Goddess go on in our hearts; merry meet, and merry part. And merry meet again. Blessed be.
- Prayer, my longing for fresh waters.

Chapter 10: Prayers for Physical Healing
- How can I honor my body when I am sick and hurting? Ask the spirit to keep me company and pray for ease.
- Not me, not me.
- I am child of spirit. I live in a harbor of the spirit of things.
- All in its order. I work, I pray, I accept.

Part Three: Prayers for Living Your Dreams

- I am a leaf in bright color, free and ready to do its season.

- I stand with lion and bear under the sun. I am animal. I drink from the mountain spring. I am the mountain. I am the spring. I sit, dance, hunt, and eat. I am the arrow that finds my mark.

Chapter 11: Prayers for Moving Into the Unknown

- You were welcomed to us as a beloved child and now you have grown. You are strong and have learned much, active and moving as the mountain streams, changeable as the air over water. We wish you long life. We wish you love. We wish you wisdom to ask for help and to learn more every year. We give to you the world we have helped make and ask you to be a shapemaker of tomorrow. We ask you to know you are human, a part of all things. We ask you to know you are human, a part of us all.
- Let it happen, a woman changed into grace.
- I pray for sparklers and the gentle calm.
- My experience, my journey of hope and healing.

Chapter 12: Freeing Your Imagination

- I changed by remembering.
- Let imagination better my life.
- We pray for transformation of what is in our control.

Chapter 13: Signposts: The Symbols of Life

- I can see. Help me see.
- Moon, shaper of change and renewal, hear our prayer. Sun, the center and heart of the sky, feel our heart. Tree of life, for us, for me. Pear, round and healthy, great health and hope. Desert, twin of desolation and contemplation, hold life bright.
- My heart to the heart of the world.

- Help me believe. Tie my life with meaning. Let me find a way.
- We are life without end, like the circle everlasting.
- I am all these: the china hand that feeds me, the long-legged bird that waddles her way through the mud flats, the shore bird in her white dress that comes to find warmth in the harbor. I am the book whose pages hold knowledge, the poem that holds the pulse of the heart, wisdom in the shape of a tiny bell.

Chapter 14: Mining the World of Dreams

- In the earth, the answers. In the earth, the prayer. I pray to know my true nature. I pray to know my ground.
- Let wisdom start here with the shimmering pearl.
- How soft the rain falls as it creates life and fills the waters.
- Let me be in the bustle of everyday.
- Resting for now, enough to do.
- I want to breathe fresh air.

Chapter 15: Creating a Vision

- I am this person who bullies and who is sorry. I don't really don't know how to stop. Help me learn cooperation and understand that I am all things: the bully, the underdog, the cooperative person. Let me choose cooperation. Let me choose love.
- Yes. Me. All of me including this.
- Spirit, I offer myself to your care. Show me the way, allow me to follow a nature most deeply mine. Help me create a larger vision of myself.
- Free and committed, continued happiness.
- Here I am. Happy and teaching.
- I wish for the best for all of us.

Chapter 16: Saying Yes
- Opportunity, everywhere.
- I am becoming more and more myself.
- Guide me to my best self. Let me say yes to possibilities. Let me feel hope.
- Beginning again, room for silence, room for dream.
- I am a ripple in the sea. I belong to the whole. Guide me.
- I ask for circles of healing, the heartbeat, the planet in the mantle of love.

Chapter 17: Helping Prayer Work
- One with you, One with you.
- I'm coming to you as I come to myself.
- Help me see my part. As I forgive myself, I forgive. As I forgive, I forgive myself.
- Let me know when I'm ready.
- Let me be a more accepting person. Let my anger be considered. May I believe I am a good person. May I believe I can take care of myself well. May I trust that I can be in a caring community of friends.
- I will know when I know.

Chapter 18: Everyday a Source of Prayer
- Lessons everywhere, and god.
- In the light, blessed be.
- Bless this child. Hold him.
- Let love heal.
- I believe.
- Let me smell the sweet smell of flowers.
- Let the best happen. Protect us. Let me be led. Watch over the deeply wounded in the world, please God, dear mother.

- Thank you, spirit, for the peace of today in me and around me.
- How can I help?
- Let good be everywhere – a waterfall – the fish flying their silver through it, the water before it and the water behind it, a gentle lapping near people who live with its cleansing and take life from its mouth.
- I rest like the field – dormant, replenishing. Silence is a song. I'm held by life. Quietly, life lives inside of me.
- Let me know everything. Let me know everything. Let me ride the pony down to the creek behind the barn.
- Silence like snow holds.
- Thank you for the world at my fingertips. Mother, father, nature, room for all.
- May I open my heart to the rich soil of my life.

Part Four: Tipping the Balance

Chapter 19: Action as Prayer

- You there, you are my sister. You there, you are my brother. You are my family and I bring you into my heart. You are my family and I feel your heart.
- I want to be part of my time. When I'm ready, let prayer lead me to involvement.
- Brothers and sisters, all.
- How can I make a difference? How can I most be me?
- Thank you for the beauty in this care group. Thank you for their laughter and warm food.
- Count on me in sweet contentment.
- Human family, blessed be.

- I offer myself in the ways that I can.
- I'm glad you're free. I ask to be brought to awareness so I cause no harm.
- My prayer, I am not done in my hope.

Chapter 20: Praying for Others
- Let the best happen. Let _____ be helped.
- Help my friends. Help all people.
- Let her ankle totally heal.
- Hop, skip, and jump with me in Yosemite woods.
- Let me hop and skip and jump in Yosemite this summer.
- I care. I want the best for you. You are in my heart. I wish you well. I care for you.

Chapter 21: Praying with Others
- Hearts beating together, spirits alive.
- I feel the rumbles in the weather of my being.

Chapter 22: Praying for Love of Country and the World
- Blessed be the victim, the dead and injured. Help us all.
- We are one. Human.
- Let me be part of the solution.
- May strength and wisdom enter our healing. May cooperation reign. May the hurt be held in the arms of care. May good rise from the ash.
- Let there be a new beginning.
- Let us be all things.
- Let us be united in grief. Guide us. Reflective consideration. Temperate action. Spirit, be with us.
- Healing after grief, forgiveness after disaster.

- As we touch life, may our actions be guided.
- I am sorry. I am sorry for you and your loved ones.
- Other ways. Possibilities of peace that last.
- Allow our hearts to open to listen. Let us understand all sides.
- I let my voice be heard. Peace in me. Peace in you. Peace all around us. Peace for all of us. We are enveloped in peace. No war for profit. Peace for all. I am a part of my times. I help create a peaceful family. I help create a peaceful workplace. I help create a peaceful community. I help create a peaceful world.
- I hold good in my heart for the people of our country and the world.
- See us now, open to the vastness of life.
- I long for a community of kind hearts to walk the days with me, reminding and nurturing the best in me. Let the group start with me.
- All people, all things living for good.

Chapter 23: Prayers for the Earth That is a Part of Us
- Let me step into the circle. Let me step into the circle of life.
- This is what I want to happen, that our earth mother be clothed in ground snow in rest before the time of seed and planting, then the season of blossom and fruit. That fire clear the forest but just enough, the birds gathering thistle, willow, and cottonwood, the mountain shielding the valley from the winds and too much rain, the spruce growing in the shade of aspen, fir in the shade of yellow pine. Into the bodies of stars and the round bright sun, life beamed, given and returned to the sky. I give this prayer, my drum alive.
- I am the world, myself, all living beings.
- Water, oceans of my life.
- I remember you.

- Together we belong.
- All of us, forest and fish, human, together – treasures.
- Let peace begin with me. Let me be an instrument. Let me be the voice of peace. Let peace begin with me.
- More than kindness know, let me in kindness act. Let me find my way to children's door so that I may find in the full smile of their face a healing force. Let me find a child who needs a sewn bear and warm milk. The human spirit longs for peace among the flocks and together we share our cupped hands.
- I live on this earth with grace and caring.
- Just to start begins it all.
- Our prayer: always the human race, our family circle, the bird and the bear, hollyhocks and forget-me-nots – one embrace – the mud body of earth.